EVOLUTION OF HINDU MORAL IDEALS

KAMALA DEVI

KAMALA LECTURES

EVOLUTION OF HINDU MORAL IDEALS

By

Sir P. S. Sivaswamy Aiyer

GYAN

Published by

GYAN

Gyan Publishing House
5, Ansari Road
Daryaganj, New Delhi-110002
Phone: 011-47034999, 9811692060
E-mail: books@gyanbooks.com

Distribution Network
gyanbooks.com
India, USA, Canada, UK, Australia, France

ISBN : 978-81-212-6609-3 (PB)
First Published, 1935

2nd Impression 2022

Printed at: Gyan Press, Delhi.

EVOLUTION OF HINDU MORAL IDEALS
Author: SIR P. S. SIVASWAMY AIYER

KAMALA LECTURES

EVOLUTION OF HINDU MORAL IDEALS

BY

SIR P. S. SIVASWAMY AIYER, K.C.S.I., C.I.E., LL.D.

1935

SIR ASUTOSH MOOKERJEE
(The Founder)

FOUNDER'S LETTER

77, Russa Road North,
Bhowanipore,
Calcutta.
9th February, 1924.

To

The Registrar,
Calcutta University.

Sir,

I desire to place at the disposal of my University Government Securities for Rupees Forty Thousand only of the 3 per cent. loan with a view to establish a lectureship, to be called the *Kamala Lectureship*, in memory of my beloved daughter (*b.* 18th April, 1895—*d.* 4th January, 1923). The Lecturer, who will be annually appointed by the Senate, will deliver a course of not less than three lectures, either in Bengali or in English, on some aspect of Indian Life and Thought, the subject to be treated from a comparative standpoint.

The following scheme shall be adopted for the lectureship:—

(1) Not later than the 31st March every year, a Special Committee of five members shall be constituted as follows:

One member of the Faculty of Arts to be nominated by the Faculty.

One member of the Faculty of Science to be nominated by the Faculty.

One member to be nominated by the Council of the Asiatic Society of Bengal.

One member to be nominated by the Bangiya Sahitya Parishad.

One member to be nominated by the Founder or his representatives.

(2) The Special Committee, after such enquiry as they may deem necessary, shall, not later than the 30th June, draw up a report recommending to the Senate the name of a distinguished scholar. The report shall specify the subject of the proposed lectures and shall include a brief statement of their scope.

(3) The report of the Special Committee shall be forwarded to the Syndicate in order that it may be laid before the Senate for confirmation not later than the 31st July.

(4) The Senate may, for specified reasons, request the Special Committee to reconsider their decision, but shall not be competent to substitute another name for the one recommended by the Committee.

(5) The Lecturer appointed by the Senate shall deliver the lectures at the Senate House not later than the month of January next following.

(6) The Syndicate shall, after the lectures are delivered in Calcutta, arrange to have them deli-

vered in the original or in a modified form in at least one place out of Calcutta, and shall, for this purpose, pay such travelling allowance as may be necessary.

(7) The honorarium of the Lecturer shall consist of a sum of Rupees One Thousand in cash and a Gold Medal of the value of Rupees Two Hundred only. The honorarium shall be paid only after the lectures have been delivered and the Lecturer has made over to the Registrar a complete copy of the lectures in a form ready for publication.

(8) The lectures shall be published by the University within six months of their delivery and after defraying the cost of publication, the surplus sale proceeds shall be paid to the Lecturer, in whom the copyright of the lectures shall vest.

(9) No person who has once been appointed a Lecturer shall be eligible for re-appointment before the lapse of five years.

Yours faithfully,

ASUTOSH MOOKERJEE.

SIR P. S. SIVASWAMY AIYER
(*The Lecturer*)

PREFACE.

The terms of the Kamalā lectureship require the delivery of a course of not less than three lectures on some aspect of Indian life and thought from a comparative standpoint. When I was approached by Mr. Syama Prasad Mookerjee, the present Vice-Chancellor, with a request to deliver a course of Kamalā lectures, he suggested that I might deal with the future constitution of India. I was reluctant to deal with a subject which was involved in great uncertainty and controversy and at a time when the whole constitution was in the melting pot. Mr. Mookerjee was kind enough to leave the choice of the subject entirely to my discretion and merely expressed a desire that the subject should be one of living, and not purely academic, interest. I accordingly chose the 'Evolution of Hindu Moral Ideals' as the subject of my lectures. While from the academic point of view the subject is one of great interest to the student of social history, it has also a valuable practical bearing upon some of the problems which affect the social life and evolution of India. An adequate treatment of the history of morals among the Hindus would require many years of preparation by way of study and research and the learning and historical gifts of Lecky. The task would be a stupendous one far beyond the range of ambition of a humble student like myself. The task that I have set to myself is one of a much more limited scope. It has been suggested to me by certain tendencies in Indian thought which have taken shape in the Sanātanist movement of the last ten or fifteen years. Since the inauguration of the Montagu-Chelmsford reforms the Indian legislature has displayed an active interest in the promotion of social reform among Hindus by means of legislation. The attack made upon social usages and the rules of Hindu law by the reforming zeal and ambition of members of the legislature has naturally created a feeling of alarm in orthodox Hindu circles. The desire to protect the personal laws and social usages of the Hindu community has led to the formation of a Sanātanist group in the legislature and of Sanātana Dharma associations in the country. The object of these groups and associations is to resist the onslaughts of the social reformers and they take their stand on an appeal to the principles of the Dharma Śāstra which they contend are eternal and immutable. It is easy to understand and appreciate the fears of the orthodox party which are not altogether without foundation. Our legislatures are composed of men of different religious creeds and it is by no means an unreasonable demand that questions affecting the personal laws or social usages of the Hindu community should not be disposed of by a heterogeneous legislature including members of alien creeds ill-equipped by knowledge or sympathy to appreciate the problems affecting the life of another community. That legislation affecting the social life of one religious community should not be carried through by the votes of members of other communities is one thing. That no changes should be carried out at all by recourse to legislation is quite another thing. The circumstances under which the legislature may interfere in matters of social reform are not so much in need of precise definition in a country which enjoys a democratic or responsible form of government free from the complications of minority problems. But in a country like India where the legislature has not yet become democratic or responsible and is composed of members of various creeds, the interference of the legislature has to be exercised more cautiously. The question which a legislature has to consider in matters of this sort is whether the society on whose behalf a proposal is made for a change is ripe for it and whether the change is supported by the bulk of public opinion. There may be cases in which a legislature which is bureaucratic or semi-responsible may be justified in enacting laws which are in advance of the public opinion of the society concerned. But such cases must be exceptional and they can only be justified on the ground that the change is necessary for the suppression of inhuman, immoral or cruel practices, or that the existing rule or usage is injurious to the moral or physical well-being of the nation, or is a violation of individual liberty not compensated by a greater public good. The prohibition of Satī, of the dedication of girls to temples as Devadāsīs or the legalisation of the re-marriage of Hindu widows can be justified on such grounds. But ordinarily legislation which is much in advance of public opinion is bound to be a failure.

The position taken by the Sanātanists goes very much further than the necessities of the case. They are opposed in principle to any interference by the legislature in matters affecting the personal laws and usages of the Hindu community. The assumptions underlying this position are that the rules and principles laid down in the Dharma Śāstras are eternal and immutable and should not be subject to any interference by the legislature. An examination of the history of the rules contained in the Dharma Śāstras and the personal laws and usages of the people is necessary to see how far these assumptions are well-founded. The present movement for maintaining the rules of Sanātana Dharma in their integrity is a defensive movement of Hindu orthodoxy reacting to the forces of social reform. This revivalist movement is very similar to the growth of fundamentalism in America since the Great War and is of the same retrograde character. It would be impossible to contend that the rules contained in the Dharma Śāstras have undergone no change or evolution in the course of ages. Even if the rules contained in the Dharma Śāstras have hitherto undergone no change, it would be no argument against any change in the future, should there be any necessity for it. But as a matter of fact the rules of the Dharma Śāstras and the Hindu ethical ideals have undergone change from time to time in accordance with the exigencies of the times. The questions which I have undertaken to consider in the course of these lectures are whether the Hindu ethical code has been rigid or flexible, whether it has been stationary and can afford to remain so or has been affected by our environments, political and economic conditions and other factors. I have also dealt with the question whether the changes in our rules and ideals have been beneficial or otherwise, whether our social structure is likely to remain stable under the impact of Western ideas and what are the tendencies of the forces at work now among us.

Another consideration which has influenced me in the choice of my subject is that frequent attacks have been recently made by Christian writers on the principles of Hinduism with the object of showing that the ethical and social progress of India has been retarded by the essential principles of Hinduism. The criticism of these writers is generally ill-informed and unfair and often inspired by racial or religious prejudices and proceeds from a lack of historical perspective. In instituting comparisons between Eastern and Western civilisations, they do not adopt corresponding periods of time or stages in development, but indulge in a comparison between the old Hindu ideals and usages and the ideals of Europe during the last hundred years. They are blind to the defects and faults of their own system and do not make sufficient allowance for the numerous factors besides religion which have moulded the ideals and usages of the people. They are interested in proving the essential and inherent superiority of Christianity to other religions and they wish to ascribe the progress of Europe to the predominant influence of Christianity and the backwardness of the East to the Eastern systems of religion. While it is impossible to deny the influence of religion on morals and the connection between the two, it is equally impossible to deny the special province of religion. As there is a tendency on the part of the Hindus to confound morals with religion, the opposite tendency of modern Christian writers is to confound religion with morals. So far as the essential principles of religion are concerned, it will be found that there is a very large measure of agreement between the great religions of the world. The matters on which they differ are precisely the matters upon which dogmatism is unjustifiable. I have briefly discussed the validity of these criticisms and examined the question whether the influence of the Hindu religion has been deleterious to the ethical and social progress of India.

The limitations of the thesis I have set before myself render it unnecessary to enter into many questions which have been dealt with by writers on the evolution of morals. I have not considered it necessary to discuss the origin of our moral ideas in biological instincts or in the social customs and practices of primitive tribes. Nor have I considered it necessary to go back to the ethnical origins of Hindu society and the different streams of culture which have contributed to the formation of what is now understood as Hinduism. Equally unnecessary in my view is it to go into the question of the original Āryan and non-Āryan elements of Hindu culture and Hindu ethics. The independence of Dravidian culture and Dravidian influence has been very warmly insisted upon in recent times. While the originally distinct existence of the Dravidian people may be conceded, it may be safely said that at no known period within historical times have the Dravidian people been unaffected by their intercourse with the Āryans and by Āryan literature and culture. It is sufficient for the purposes of our inquiry to take Hindu society as it has existed during the last 2,500 years and more, since the time it acquired the consciousness of a common social structure, common religious beliefs and common moral ideals.

A satisfactory treatment of the subject would require a division of the history into successive well-defined epochs. They may be divided into ancient, mediæval and modern, or the ages of the Vedas, Sūtras and Smṛtis, the classical and Purāṇic period and the period of the digests of Hindu law composed in later times. Mr. P. V. Kane divides the Dharma Śāstra literature into three periods, the first coming down to the Christian era, the second covering the first eight centuries of the Christian era and the third beginning with the ninth and ending with the eighteenth century. I have not found it necessary for my purpose to attempt any scientific division of the epochs of history. Any sharp definition of epochs is not practicable in the case of the history of any country and in the case of ancient India the want of satisfactory chronological data presents a serious obstacle. The dates assigned to important writers and treatises by different scholars differ very considerably and the margin of variation in their estimates sometimes extends to a period of four or five centuries, if not more. By way of illustration I need only refer to the great divergence among scholars with regard to the dates to be assigned to Manu, Āpastamba, Bodhāyana, the *Rāmāyaṇa,* the *Mahābhārata* and the *Arthaśāstra* of Kauṭilya. I have considered it unnecessary for my purpose to enter into these vexed questions of chronology. There is a certain amount of rough agreement among scholars as to the sequence in time of the more important treatises and it is easy to prove changes in moral conceptions and legal rules during the centuries for which there is available literature. The history of the ethical ideals of Hindus presents two striking features. They have not remained stationary, but have changed in various directions from time to time. Secondly, there is no breach of continuity in the main web of Indian culture. There have been no catastrophic changes marking off one period from its predecessor. Nor can it be said of any particular change that it is not the result of a natural process of evolution or due to the germs of change inherent in the Hindu system of thought and culture. It must be remembered that from the very earliest times the widest possible latitude was given to speculations in the fields of religion and ethics and divergent schools have flourished in both these fields. The influence of foreign culture is to be traced not so much in the introduction of absolutely new ideas as in the stress laid upon particular ideas already at work or in the acceleration of the process of change.

As regards the topics to be included in my inquiry, I have not attempted any scientific classification. Whatever may be the principle of classification adopted, the topics will be found to be closely connected with each other and very often interdependent. I have dealt with many of the topics usually treated by writers on the evolution of morals. It is not possible to deal in great detail with any of these various topics. Each of them would require a separate treatise for a full account. A detailed history of each of these topics is not possible within the compass of the lectures contemplated by the foundation and would besides have involved an enormous amount of labour which I could not possibly attempt.

In conclusion I have to express my high appreciation of the honour which the Calcutta University has done me in inviting me to deliver a course of the Kamalā Lectures, an honour for which I feel indebted to the initiative of Mr. Syama Prasad Mookerjee, the son of the founder and a member of the Syndicate at the time of the invitation.

I have in the body of the book given references to the works upon which I have drawn. It is necessary, however, to make special mention of three treatises to which I am specially indebted and which no writer on the history of morals can afford to neglect: I refer to W. E. H. Lecky's *History of European Morals*, E. Westermarck's *Origin and Development of the Moral Ideas* and L. T. Hobhouse's *Morals in Evolution*. I have also derived help from Mr. Maganlal A. Buch's *Principles of Hindu Ethics* which is a storehouse of citations from the Dharma Śāstras and other literature bearing upon the subject.

My grateful thanks are due to Prof. S. Kuppuswami Sastri and Pandit S. K. Padmanabha Sastri of the Presidency College, Madras, who have readily given me the benefit of their great learning on all points on which I consulted them. I am further indebted to Prof. Kuppuswami Sastri for having kindly looked over the typescript and proof sheets of my lectures. I have also to acknowledge my obligations to Mr. A. B. Dhruva, the Pro. Vice-Chancellor of the Benares Hindu University, and to Sir S. Radhakrishnan, the Vice-Chancellor of the Andhra University, who found time to read the typescript of my lectures and offered helpful comments.

It gives me great pleasure to acknowledge the valuable and ungrudging help I have received from my clerk V. Duraiswami throughout the preparation of these lectures in verifying the references, preparing the book for the press and revising the proofs. The labour of preparing the index has been kindly shared by him and Mr. T. R. Chintamani,

Senior Lecturer in Sanskrit in the Madras University. To both of them I tender my sincere thanks.

Finally I have to express my high appreciation of the quality of the work done by the Madras Law Journal Press, to whose proprietor, Mr. R. Narayanaswami Iyer, I offer my best thanks.

P. S. S.

CONTENTS

CHAPTER I

INTRODUCTORY

THE aspect of Indian life and thought with which I propose to deal in my lectures is the "Evolution of Hindu Moral Ideals". One is confronted at the very outset with the question who are Hindus. To say that Hindus are those who follow Hinduism is no satisfactory answer. Unlike Buddhism, Christianity and Islam, Hinduism does not owe its origin to any historical person and does not connote adherence to the teaching of any particular founder. It has shown a capacity to absorb the beliefs and practices of many races and tribes, and in its endeavour to incorporate and assimilate them, it has not only exercised an influence upon the minds and habits of the peoples who were brought within its fold, but has also been influenced by its contact with them. For the purposes of the lawyer a Hindu has sometimes been defined as one who has been held by the courts to be governed by the rules of Hindu law. But this definition would include the followers of heretical or dissenting sects like the Sikhs and Jains[1] and would only take us back to the question to whom the rules of Hindu

[1]Sikhs and Jains have undoubtedly been influenced by Hindu ideals and practices. But they often object to be classed as Hindus and it is outside my purpose to enter into any controversy as to the definition of the term 'Hindu'. It is impossible to frame any definition which will not be open to criticism.

law should be applied. The rules of Hindu law applied by the courts are those originally laid down in the Sanskrit Dharma Śāstras as modified by established usages. When western scholars speak of Hindu law, they generally mean the law as laid down in the Dharma Śāstras composed by the ancient Sanskrit writers. Several writers, including some of our own countrymen, have been so impressed by the diversity of beliefs and practices among those who are called Hindus that they have confessed their inability to lay down any real test of Hinduism. A recent writer has described Hinduism as 'that all-embracing but undefinable system of toleration or synthesis which shelters within its capacious bosom every form of belief and practice that will agree with its few general conventions'.[1] Other writers have been struck by the fundamental unity of thought and belief which prevails among all Hindu communities. Hinduism represents not merely a set of beliefs, but also a definite social organisation. There is perhaps not much more difficulty in defining Hindus or Hinduism than there is in defining Christians or Christianity. There are numberless sects among Christians differing from each other in doctrine and practice, and even among the votaries of any particular sect all of them do not subscribe to all the articles of faith of that sect or conform to all its practices. Nevertheless we are able to form some idea of Christianity as a whole. When western writers speak of Hinduism, they have in

[1] J. N. Sarkar: *India through the Ages*, p. 17.

mind the system of religion, philosophy, ethics and laws contained in the Sanskrit scriptures, law-books and other sacred literature. Some writers have spoken of the laws and religion as Brahminical. That they were mostly of Brahminical origin in the sense that most of the authors of the treatises were Brahmins admits of little doubt. But it would be a mistake to imagine that they were applicable only to the Brahmins and not to the other castes and classes, or that the latter were not influenced in their daily life and conduct by the beliefs, principles and ideals contained in this literature. Taking, for instance, the two great epic poems of India, there are hardly any Hindus who do not cherish the ideals set forth in these works or who have not been affected by the cultural traditions they embody. They have exercised a profound influence upon the life and thought of India. Within the last one or two generations there has been an attempt to revolt against the authority of the sacred books of Brahminical origin, an attempt due partly to communal dissensions and jealousies and partly to the influences which have been tending to the break-up of the old caste system. Notwithstanding the difficulties of framing a scientifically satisfactory definition, we can form a more or less rough conception of Hinduism as ordinarily understood. It connotes among other things belief in the authority of the Vedas and other sacred writings of the ancient sages, in the immortality of the soul and in a future life, in the existence of a Supreme God, in the theory of Karma and re-birth, in the worship of ancestors, in the social organisation represented by the four main castes, in the theory of the four stages of life and in the theory of the four Puruṣārthas or ends of human endeavour. For the purpose of the present course of lectures we may include under the term 'Hindus' those who acknowledge the authority of the Vedas and other sacred literature in Sanskrit or who have been influenced in their life and conduct by the rules, principles, ideals and culture embodied in the ancient Sanskrit literature or in the vernacular literature derived therefrom. It is my purpose to deal with the ethical ideals rather than with the practice, with the rules of conduct rather than the degree of conformity to the rules. It would, of course, not be possible entirely to separate the consideration of the rules from the consideration of actual conduct. The ethical progress of a community has to be judged more by the ideals of conduct which it sets before itself than by the extent of the conformity of its members to the ideals. Shortcomings and deviations from the rules regarded as binding are bound to occur in every society. It would be difficult to form any estimate of the proportion of the members of any society who strictly and fully conform to the requirements of the current ethical code. The ideal rule is bound to be higher than the standard of attainment and it is an advantage to society that it should be so. If, on the other hand, the ideal is so high that it cannot possibly be attained by anyone or is practically departed from by most members of the community, it cannot be treated as an accepted rule or standard. The maxim 'whosoever shall smite thee on thy right cheek, turn to him the other also' may safely be assigned to the category of impracticable ideals. Writers on the evolution of morals have therefore investigated the progress of ethical conceptions and ethical theories and do not consider it profitable to study the varying degrees in which the accepted rules of conduct have been fulfilled in practice.

It has been remarked that compared with the amount of attention given by Hindu thinkers to the subjects of religion and philosophy, the scientific study of ethics has received very little attention from them. If it is meant that there have been no systematic treatises dealing with the theory of ethics as distinguished from religion, the charge is probably true. Even in modern times the province of ethics is closely related to the provinces of law and religion. The same rules of conduct which are commended from the standpoint of morality may be adopted by the legislator as fit for inclusion in a code of laws and may be supported on religious grounds. Moral injunctions may be reinforced by legal or religious precepts and may be sanctioned by law or religion or both. The difficulty which is experienced in marking off the spheres of law, religion and ethics is far greater in the case of ancient systems and treatises. It is only in later times that a differentiation is made between these three subjects. Like the books of the Old

Testament, the old Hindu law-books mix up the topics of law, religion and ethics and claim to deal with the whole conduct of life by man. The word 'Dharma' used in Hindu literature has a very comprehensive import and our Dharma Śāstras deal with practically the whole life of man in his relations to his fellow-men, to God and to the lower animals, and claim to regulate the conduct of man in all these various relations. It includes what may be called self-regarding duties as well as duties to others, duties to deceased ancestors as well as duties to living beings. It includes the topics of Ācāra or ceremonial observances, Vyavahāra or law proper, Prāyaścitta or expiation, Āśauca or personal impurity, and a host of other topics arising out of the different situations of human life. The chapters on Ācāra are not confined to mere ritual or self-regarding duties. They include also the institutions of marriage and family. The chapter on Vyavahāra includes *inter alia* the topics of property and inheritance. We cannot exclude any of these parts of the Dharma Śāstra from our consideration, as they all afford indications of the moral ideas which underlie the different institutions and rules. Even the rules regarding Prāyaścitta or expiation which at first sight may appear to be connected with ceremonial observances furnish evidence of the moral conceptions of the community or the law-givers as to the degree of heinousness attached to the breach of different rules of conduct. The Dharma Śāstra is practically co-extensive with the whole sphere of the duties of man.

There is plenty of discussion in Hindu literature about the rules of moral conduct and about the applicability of the rules to various situations in life. The topics which are usually considered in modern ethical treatises are the standard or criterion of morality, the conceptions of good, virtue and vice, right and duty, the origin of the moral sense and the sanctions of duties. There is, of course, a great difference between the manner in which these questions have been approached by Greek or modern thinkers and the method of approach of the Hindu thinkers. While the speculations of the former are based upon the foundation of pure reason, the discussions of the latter are based upon the authority of the scriptures. Closely connected with the question of the standard or criterion of morality is the question of the sources of moral rules. This last question occupies an important place in the Hindu Dharma Śāstras. The nature and definition of Dharma, the sources of rules of Dharma and the scope and applicability of moral rules and distinctions have exercised the minds of Hindu thinkers, and Hindu literature abounds with discussions on these topics. One great difference, however, between Greek and modern thought on the one hand and Hindu thought on the other is that the Hindu is satisfied with tracing the origin of rules to some text of scripture or some authoritative tradition and does not press home the question as to the rational basis of the rule. He is satisfied with an appeal to authority and does not believe that mere unfettered intellectual reasoning can furnish guidance in matters of morality. The attempt to discover a moral standard on a rational basis has engaged the attention of modern thinkers far more than of the ancients. Hinduism is not the only system which has appealed to the standard of authority and tradition. Ordinarily the fact that a rule is derived from revelation or immemorial usage, or from supposed conformity to the law of nature, or is in accord with the enlightened conscience or the practice of the wisest and most highly esteemed members of the community, would be sufficient to set the seal of authority upon the rule. Whatever may be the actual origin and course of development of moral ideas as disclosed by a study of different stages of civilisation and culture and by a study of psychology, the aim of moralists as well as theologians has everywhere been to invest moral rules with an eternal and immutable character and not leave them to the mercy of historical accidents or the shifting currents and prejudices of social opinion. In early Greek thought traditional law was supreme not because it came from the Gods, but because it was eternal and its source was lost in the darkness out of which things come.[1] So in India the foundations of ethics were sought to be laid upon the firm rock of revelation, *i.e.*, the Śrutis or Vedas.

The supreme authority and infallibility of the Vedas or revelation was rested on the ground of their eternal character. The conclusion as to their

[1] *See* L. T. Hobhouse: *Morals in Evolution*, Vol. II, p. 185.

infallible character was arrived at in different ways by the different schools of thought and in different classes of writings. It is not necessary to refer to the accounts given by the Purāṇic and other writings which ascribe an obviously mythical origin to the Vedas. A brief reference, however, may be made to the views propounded in some of the Darśanas or systems of philosophy. The Nyāya system inferred the authority of the Veda from its being derived from an omniscient Creator or Īśvara. Among the Mīmāṁsakas there are two schools, one which admits the existence of an Īśvara or God and the other which denies it. The former school holds that Īśvara or God uttered the Veda at the beginning of each Kalpa cycle not arbitrarily and of His own sweet will and pleasure, but in accordance with His recollection of the Veda as it existed in the previous Kalpas. It therefore relies in the last resort upon immemorial tradition and the theory that the Veda had no beginning. The other school which is atheistic holds that the derivation of the authority of the Veda from its utterance by an omniscient Īśvara or God involves a vicious circle of reasoning, as the omniscience of Iśvara or God cannot be established by mere reason and can only be inferred from the Veda. It holds that any Īśvara or God, who is inferred by mere reason, cannot have the attribute of omniscience and must share the infirmities of other persons. It therefore takes the simple and straightforward step of holding that the Vedas are eternal and are of non-personal origin. The doctrine of the atheistic Sāṅkhya school is similar to that of the atheistic Mīmāṁsaka and the doctrine of the theistic Sāṅkhya school is similar to that of the theistic Mīmāṁsaka. According to the Vedāntin, the Vedas have been revealed by Īśvara, but He has revealed them from His recollection of what existed as Veda in the previous Kalpa. But whatever may be the differences between these schools, they are all agreed upon the conclusion that the Vedas are immemorial and had no beginning in time and possess an eternal character. To the modern mind the ascription of Apauruṣeyatva (non-personal or supra-human origin) or Anāditva (absence of beginning) seems absurd. But all theories and systems of belief which rest upon revelation labour more or less under the like disadvantage. The eternity of the Vedas calls only for a somewhat larger order upon belief than revelation. The reasoning by which the Hindu theologian seeks to establish the eternal character or the non-personal origin of the Śruti may be shortly stated. The Śruti has been handed down to us by immemorial tradition. It is not possible to prove that the scriptures were spoken or uttered by any particular person. As it is not possible to prove the author of the scriptures, they must be eternal. The theologian cleverly shifts the burden of proof upon his opponents, forgetting that all words and languages are of human origin and have been developed in course of time. The Vedas, however, include matter of such obviously mythical, legendary or absurd character that the Mīmāṁsaka is obliged to explain away all this matter by an elaborate science of interpretation. He divides the Vedic texts into four classes: Vidhi, Arthavāda, Mantra and Nāmadheya. The essential aim of the Śruti is either to impart knowledge of a truth otherwise unknown or to enjoin the performance of certain rites or to forbid the performance of certain acts. Texts which prescribe or prohibit are Vidhis in the larger sense. The other classes of texts are subsidiary to these. Nāmadheya texts are those which deal with nomenclature. Mantra texts have been defined as प्रयोगसमवेतार्थस्मारक, *i.e.*, those which remind us of the acts to be performed in connection with the particular Karma or rite. All other texts fall into the large category of Arthavāda, the object of which is Nindā, Praśaṁsā, Parakṛti or Purākalpa, *i.e.*, censure, praise, narratives of others' actions or statements of ancient facts. The Mīmāṁsaka holds that no authority can be attached to Arthavāda texts which are ज्ञातार्थबोधक or प्रमाणान्तरबाधितार्थबोधक, *i.e.*, which merely state facts otherwise known or facts opposed to common sense and the other canons of credibility. This rule of interpretation enables the Mīmāṁsakas and other canonical writers to explain away many passages which are of a legendary character or are opposed to common sense. For example, the texts of the Śruti which speak of sacrifices requiring a thousand years for their performance are explained away as mere Arthavāda. The *raison d'etre* and function of the Śruti, according to the Hindu theologians, is to impart knowledge which could not be obtained from other sources or to prescribe acts which would not be performed by the prompting of mere natural inclination. Otherwise the Vedas would be superfluous. No revelation, inspiration or supra-mundane authority is required to tell us things which can be learnt by the light of nature alone. At first sight this doctrine would appear to have the advantage of confining the scope and domain of the scriptures to things which are purely spiritual. But the doctrine has been applied in a manner which will surprise the modern mind and especially the minds of foreigners. Where the Śrutis enjoin the performance of particular acts for which no justification in the mere light of nature can be found, the rules are held to be valid and especially so for this reason. To discard the injunction as not binding on the ground that no earthly reason can be found for it would be a total repudiation of the validity of the scriptures. No principle of interpretation can be accepted as valid which would have the effect of abrogating the rule. The maxims of interpretation adopted by the Mīmāṁsaka show very high legal acumen and differ but little from the maxims of modern lawyers in the interpretation of statutes. It is the fault not of his principles of construction, but of his presuppositions and premises that the logical result of the Mīmāṁsaka's reasoning has been to reduce orthodoxy to a mere belief in the authority of the Vedas and in the necessity of performing the rites prescribed by them and to encourage reverence for the letter of the rule and a mechanical sacerdotalism.

The theologian's view of the purpose of the Vedas has exercised a great influence upon his conception of Dharma and of the precepts of the Dharma Śāstra. We have already remarked that the word 'Dharma' is one of very comprehensive import in Sanskrit. It is used in the senses of nature, law, justice, virtue, merit, duty and morality. It has been defined by the Mīmāṁsaka as अलौकिकश्रेयस्साधन, *i.e.*, the means of attaining welfare or happiness, where the connection between the act or omission and the consequent welfare or happiness is mysterious or not ascertainable. An act may constitute Dharma in a popular sense, but it is not Dharma according to the theologian, unless the connection between the act or omission and the resulting good is mysterious, *i.e.*, can be established only by the intervention of what is called Adṛṣṭa or Apūrva, the existence of the link being vouched only by the Śruti. It may be said that in some cases the connection between the performance of a virtuous act and the resulting happiness is obvious, as for instance when one feeds a hungry man and derives a sympathetic satisfaction from the appeasement of the other's hunger or from the consciousness of the performance of a duty. The act may be meritorious from a worldly point of view, but according to the Mīmāṁsaka this knowledge of the antecedent hunger and the subsequent satisfaction by feeding is not sufficient to constitute a knowledge of Dharma, *i.e.*, a knowledge of the mysterious spiritual merit resulting from the act of feeding. This spiritual merit may take the shape of an improvement or purification of the actor's character, disposition or mind, and may also be a means of securing welfare either in this or in a future life. It is called Adṛṣṭa because it is not obvious or visible, but mysterious, and Apūrva because it cannot be ascertained otherwise than by the Śruti. Where the connection between an act as the means of attaining a desire and its result is plain and visible, the Dharma Śāstra would be superfluous. The *raison d'etre* of the Dharma Śāstra is that it teaches us things that cannot be known otherwise. It is like faith which is the substance of things hoped for and the evidence of things not seen. It does not mean that whatever is not laid down in the Dharma Śāstra is Adharma in the sense of being opposed to Dharma, or wrong, vicious or evil. The Mīmāṁsā of Jaimini therefore lays down that Dharma is चोदनालक्षण, *i.e.*, that what is Dharma or the reverse can only be ascertained from the injunctions, positive or negative, of the Vedas. This peculiar conception of Dharma, based as it is upon the authority of the eternal Vedas and the necessity for placing the rules of conduct on a supra-sensible basis, has tended to the entanglement of ethics with religion and rendered it difficult to extricate ethics from religious theory. Highly artificial as this theory is and however curious may appear to us the mental attitude which resents the intrusion of reason in any inquiry as to the validity of the precepts of the Dharma Śāstra, it is comforting to find that the ethical rules laid down by the Hindu scriptures are generally in accord with the notions of morality accepted in civilised communities. The process may look strange and devious, but the results are generally right.

Though the Vedas are held to be the ultimate foundation of our knowledge of Dharma, there are also available other sources which have a derivative validity. According to the Dharma Śāstras, the sources of our knowledge of Dharma are the Vedas, the Smṛtis, the practice of the virtuous and the approval of an enlightened conscience.[1] These sources are supposed to be of unquestionable authority and the inquiry whether their authority rests upon any underlying principle or criterion is not encouraged. The *ipse dixit* of the Dharma Śāstra

1 वेदोऽखिलो धर्ममूलं स्मृतिशीले च तद्विदाम् ।
आचारश्चैव साधूनामात्मनस्तुष्टिरेव च ॥
वेदः स्मृतिः सदाचारः स्वस्य च प्रियमात्मनः ।
एतच्चतुर्विधं प्राहुः साक्षाद्धर्मस्य लक्षणम् ॥

Manu, II, 6, 12.

श्रुतिः स्मृतिः सदाचारः स्वस्य च प्रियमात्मनः ।
सम्यक् सङ्कल्पजः कामो धर्ममूलमिदं स्मृतम् ॥
पुराणन्यायमीमांसाधर्मशास्त्राङ्गमिश्रिताः ।
वेदाः स्थानानि विद्यानां धर्मस्य च चतुर्दश ॥
मन्वत्रिविष्णुहारीतयाज्ञवल्क्योशनोऽङ्गिराः ।
यमापस्तम्बसंवर्ताः कात्यायनबृहस्पती ॥
पराशरव्यासशङ्खलिखिता दक्षगौतमौ ।
शातातपो वसिष्ठश्च धर्मशास्त्रप्रयोजकाः ॥

Yājñavalkya, I, 7, 3-5.

is sufficient for the orthodox Hindu. The justification for the position is that reason is no certain or infallible guide, that variations of opinion are innumerable and that it is impossible to arrive at any certainty with regard to any rule of conduct by the light of mere reason. This view ignores the large measure of agreement on moral rules in civilised communities, exaggerates diversities and ascribes impotence to reason. A firm basis for Dharma having been laid on the eternal scriptures, it is declared that the rules of Dharma are eternal and immutable. The rejection of reason and experience as a guide to morality may cause some surprise. But this view is not very much removed from that of the intuitional school of moralists who consider it necessary to postulate a special moral faculty for the perception of right and wrong. It would be clear from the foregoing remarks why there have been no systematic treatises on the theory of ethics in Sanskrit literature and why ethical discussions stop short with the texts of the Dharma Śāstras.

According to strict theory, the rules of conduct laid down in the Dharma Śāstras are supposed to be eternal and immutable. But have they in fact undergone no change? It would be surprising if in the long course of ages rules of conduct formulated hundreds and thousands of years ago remained unchanged. Adaptation to changes of environment is the essential condition of life. It would be impossible to suggest that there have been no changes in our external environments or that there has been no necessity for re-examination and revision of moral rules or that there have in fact been no alterations in moral rules. While paying lip-homage to the eternal and immutable character of Sanātana Dharma, the commentators on the Śāstras have generally endeavoured to bring them into relation and accordance with the conditions of the society in which they lived. The Hindu mind has never been lacking in legal subtlety and the commentators upon our Śāstras have had no difficulty, by recourse to the principles of interpretation and to legal fictions, in bringing about such modifications in the rules as society stood in need of. It is not intended to suggest that there are no moral principles of universal or more or less general validity, but only that the moral code has not been stationary, and has undergone evolution. It can be shown that even according to the Dharma Śāstras there have been such variations and adjustments to meet changes of external conditions. This will be seen by reference to the variations of Yuga Dharma,[1] to the practices allowed or forbidden in the present age (Kaliyuga), to the recognition of local usages and the usages of particular castes and classes, to the rules of Āpad-dharma or Dharma during distress and adversity and to the principle of accommodation to the ability of a person for performance,[2]

[1] *Manu*, I, 85.

[2] "आख्यातानामर्थं ब्रुवतां शक्तिः सहकारिणी" (See *Śābarabhāṣya* on Mīmāṃsā-darśana, I, iv, 30) corresponding to the maxim *lex non cogit ad impossibilia* (The law does not prescribe impossible things).

as illustrated in the case of the curtailment of the period of Vedic study or Brahmacarya. The differences in rules in different Śākhās and Sūtras must also have been brought about not as a mere intellectual sport, but probably in recognition of some local custom or requirement. Economic conditions must have necessarily affected social institutions and ethical rules. In the course of my lectures I shall deal with the actual rules formulated and recognised from time to time to meet changes in conditions, rather than with the specific theories or reasons advanced in support of the changes.

A historical inquiry into the subject of the evolution of moral ideals is beset with difficulties due to the absence of adequate data, the absence of the historical sense among the Hindus, their disregard for chronology and the absurd attempt of the Hindu writers on Dharma Śāstra to ascribe equal validity to all Smṛti writers irrespective of age or epoch. They refuse to recognise any successive stratification of the Dharma Śāstra works, but when it suits them, they treat the earlier ordinances as applicable only to a former age (Yuga) and the later ordinances as specially applicable to the present age. The sage Parāśara who is supposed to be a special Smṛti writer of the Kali age is obeyed only when his precepts are in accord with present day customs and prejudices and coolly disregarded when his rules are not in accord with current customs and prejudices. Our inquiry has therefore to be made in the light of such historical data as have been made available by modern research. According to the Smṛti of Yājñavalkya,[1] the chief writers on Dharma Śāstra are Manu, Atri, Viṣṇu, Hārīta, Yājñavalkya, Uśanas, Aṅgiras, Yama, Āpastamba, Saṁvarta, Kātyāyana, Bṛhaspati, Parāśara, Vyāsa, Śaṅkha, Likhita, Dakṣa, Gautama, Śātātapa and Vasiṣṭha. This is not, however, an exhaustive list. It makes no reference, for instance, to Bodhāyana and Nārada. The chronological lists of Dharma Śāstra writers prepared by modern scholars do not all tally. But these divergent estimates are only what must be expected from the absence of history and biography and other conclusive chronological data.

It cannot possibly be suggested even by the most orthodox that the Smṛti writers all lived at the same time. One would naturally imagine that the work of each writer was composed with reference to the province to which he belonged and to the conditions and customs obtaining when he lived. They are supposed to be all equally authoritative for the reason that they are all based upon the Śruti. The assumption made by all the Smṛti writers is that the Śruti is the ultimate source of all our knowledge of Dharma. Unfortunately for this assumption the existing Vedas deal with only a very small portion of the topics treated in the Smṛtis. The Yajurveda deals mostly with sacrificial ritual; the Ṛg Veda is mostly concerned with hymns to Gods; and the Sāma Veda is mostly a collection of the texts intended for singing at the

[1] *Yājñavalkya*, I, 4-5.

sacrifices. The Upaniṣads are mainly concerned with problems of metaphysics and it is only very rarely that one meets with moral rules as in the case of the *Taittirīya Upaniṣad.* On the other hand, the topics dealt with in the Dharma Śāstra are numerous and varied and the treatises descend to the minutest details of life and conduct. To search for the source of all the Smṛti rules in the Vedas is simply to search for something which is not there. But the ingenuity of the commentator is not baffled by this circumstance. If no text of the Śruti in support of the Smṛti rule can be found, he has recourse to the fiction that a Śruti text must be inferred or assumed in support of the Smṛti. Like the English lawyer who had recourse to the fiction of a lost grant, the Hindu legist assumes that the Śruti text might have been lost or forgotten. The fiction of a lost or forgotten Śruti text in support of a Smṛti rule is vigorously attacked by the critic in the *Tantra Vartika* and his arguments meet with a very feeble reply from the author Kumārila. A halo of sanctity is spread over all the rules, important or trivial, by the fiction that they are all derived from the Vedas. If there are conflicting passages in a single treatise, an attempt to reconcile them is justified. But where there are conflicting rules in treatises composed at different epochs, attempts to reconcile them are beset with numerous difficulties. The divergences of Śruti texts and of law-givers were a source of perplexity even in the age of the *Mahābhārata* and Yudhiṣṭhira complained that the secret of Dharma was hidden and that the only safe course was to follow the usages of the people.[1] In the introduction to his commentary on the *Parāśara Smṛti* the famous Mādhavācārya says that rules of the Śāstras vary with the country, with the time and according to the ability of persons for compliance with the rules, and that commentators of the Smṛtis who attempt to reconcile and settle the meaning of varying texts do so merely for the practical guidance of the unintelligent.[2] A modern lawyer who is called upon to decide upon the validity of conflicting enactments would be disposed to apply the rule that the later expression of the will of the legislature must be held to overrule the earlier. This course is not open to the Hindu commentator who attaches very little value to the chronological sequence of the law-givers, and it is not surprising that his efforts are often unsatisfactory and unsuccessful. He is often obliged to introduce all sorts of unworkable distinctions in laying down under what circumstances one rule or the other is to be applied. For instance, with regard to the case of the extra share to be given to an eldest son on the partition of the family property, there are

[1] तर्कोऽप्रतिष्ठः श्रुतयो विभिन्ना
नैको ऋषिर्यस्य मतं प्रमाणम् ।
धर्मस्य तत्त्वं निहितं गुहायां
महाजनो येन गतः स पन्थाः ॥

Vanaparva, 313, 117.

My translation follows the commentary of Nilakaṇṭha. But the word महाजन is also interpreted as meaning the good or the great.

[2] *See* Bombay Sanskrit Series, XLVII, Vol. I, Part I, pp. 26-27.

texts which prescribe an extra share and there are others which prohibit it. The natural historical explanation would be that the first rule was a vestige of the patriarchal system and that the second rule was laid down after the break-up of the patriarchal system. The explanation of the commentators is that the texts recognising an extra share refer to cases of superior merit on the part of the eldest son. How this superior merit should be ascertained and by whom is not a question which troubles the commentators. It is sufficient for them that they have recognised both the texts as equally authoritative. The loyalty which the commentators profess to the Vedas is neither consistent nor genuine. If the Vedas contemplate only post-puberty marriage and the later Smṛti writers prescribe the marriage of girls who have not attained puberty, the authority of the Vedas is quietly ignored and it is said that the earlier rules were intended to be applied to a previous Yuga. If the later writers prohibit the performance of Vedic sacrifices in the present age, the rule is set aside in favour of the earlier rules which enjoin the performance of sacrifices as a duty of the householder. Generally speaking, the tendency of a modern court is to construe doubtful passages in statutes in favour of the liberty of the subject. But the tendency of the old Hindu commentator is to adopt a restrictive interpretation. Where the rule of an older Smṛti is in favour of freedom and a later rule restricts such freedom, as for example in the case of inter-marriage between castes, the commentator has recourse to the theory that the earlier rule is inapplicable on account of the degeneracy of the human race and the moral inferiority of the present generation to the older. The complaint of degeneracy goes back to the earliest times and there has hardly ever been an age before what may be called the modern period of history when people did not complain of the moral degeneracy of the times in which they lived.[1] Udayanācārya who lived in the tenth century A.D. complained of the degenerate habits of the Brahmins in his time in regard to occupation, livelihood and sex relations. Having regard to the different dates at which the works on Dharma Śāstra were composed, it is obvious that in former times the later writers were admitted from time to time into the category of authoritative law-givers. Why this process of recognition should not be continued to the present day is not intelligible except on the theory of the degeneracy of the modern age and its consequent incompetency for legislation. India is not the only country in which antiquity has conferred a superior claim to sanctity. Notwithstanding the conservatism of the interpreters of the law and their disposition to rely upon ancient authority, they were compelled by force of circumstances to recognise the changes that had crept into the life of the people. The Hindu law has not in fact been as rigid and stagnant as might have been expected from the theory of the law-books.

[1]*See* the description of Yuga Dharmas in *Mahābhārata, Vanaparva,* 149; *Śāntiparva,* 69; *Bhīṣmaparva,* 10.

CHAPTER II

CHANGES IN ETHICO-LEGAL CONCEPTIONS

We shall now proceed to a survey of the changes in the moral conceptions underlying the social life of the Hindus. Two of the most deeply rooted institutions in the structure of society in all parts of the world and especially in India are the family and property. We shall therefore begin our survey with an account of the changes that have taken place in the rules governing these institutions and the moral sentiments associated with them.

Marriage.

There are eight forms of marriage referred to by Manu and other ancient law-givers: Brāhma, Daiva, Arṣa, Prājāpatya, Āsura, Gāndharva, Rākṣasa and Paiśāca.[1] It is obvious that some of these forms relate to a very primitive state of society and picture a very low ideal of the institution of marriage. The Paiśāca form which was considered the basest could hardly have been recognised as a lawful form of marriage in any civilised society. The only reason for its inclusion in the list of forms of marriage was probably the desire of the writers for completeness of the catalogue. The Rākṣasa form of marriage by capture has long since fallen into disuse. The Gāndharva form which arose out of mere amorous intercourse has also become obsolete. It was laid

[1] *Manu,* III, 21.

down by some Smṛti writers that this marriage could not be recognised as valid, unless the original union was followed by the performance of the usual marriage ceremonies.[1] The only two forms of marriage now extant are the Brāhma and Asura forms. The latter, which involves the payment of a price for the bride, has been rightly condemned by Manu as immoral.

Though polygyny is permitted by the Hindu law, the ideal was monogamy. The first marriage alone was regarded as contracted in the performance of a religious duty and any subsequent marriage was regarded as merely the result of desire and not of a sense of duty. Though polygyny obtains in the families of ruling princes and zamindars and among the Kulin Brahmins of Bengal and the Nambūdris of Malabar,[2] it is not common among other classes of people. It is only when the first wife is barren or has no male issue or is adulterous or diseased, that a second wife is married. Public opinion has been steadily undergoing a change in favour of monogamy as the result of education, economic pressure and recognition of the just claims of women.

As regards the age of marriage, there can be no doubt that during the Vedic period the marriage of girls who had not attained the age of puberty

[1] *Devala Smṛti* and *Gṛhya Pariśiṣṭa* quoted in *Parāśara Mādhavīya* (Bombay Sanskrit Series), Vol. I, Part II, p. 89. *See also* I.L.R. 12 Madras 72.

[2] Madras Act XXI of 1933 has set the stamp of disapproval on the marriage of a second wife during the lifetime of the first, except in three cases.

was not contemplated at all. The Vedic Mantras employed in the marriage ceremonies clearly show that the parties to the marriage were capable of consummating the marriage immediately after the ceremonies. The age of marriage for girls had been lowered by the time when the Sūtras and the Smṛtis were composed. The vast majority of the Smṛtis inculcate the marriage of girls below puberty. There is no similar injunction in the case of males that they should be married before puberty. The ordinary rule in the case of a male of the twice-born classes was that he was to enter upon the duties of a householder after he completed the period of his studentship which would not take place before he attained majority. The reasons for the introduction of the practice of child-marriage cannot be definitely assigned. Probably it was the result of many factors such as the gradual decline in the status of women and the growing assertion of authority by men over women and children, the desire to procure suitable husbands within the limited circle permitted by the rules of endogamy, the fear that if girls were not married before puberty they might claim a right of self-determination in the choice of their husbands, the great importance attached to virginity and the desire to prevent any temptations or dangers likely to lead to a loss of it. Another reason suggested by Rai Bahadur C. V. Vaidya for child-marriages is the fear of parents that their girls might enter a Buddhist nunnery.[1] Though the marriage of girls before

[1]*History of Medieval India*, Vol. II, p. 189.

puberty is inculcated in the Smṛtis, they do not go the length of declaring the marriage of a girl after puberty to be invalid. There are several texts which recognise the validity of post-puberty marriages. If a girl is not given in marriage by her parents or guardians before puberty, she is required to wait for three years and then choose a husband for herself.[1] The gift of a girl in marriage before puberty is a duty laid upon her parents or guardians and a failure to comply with it is sinful on their part. But neither the girl herself nor her husband incurs any sin or reproach[2] and her marriage is lawful. Even in the case of the parent, he is not obliged to give his daughter in marriage, if he is not able to procure a suitable husband. Manu distinctly declares that a maiden, though marriageable, should rather stop in her father's house until death and that the father should never give her to a man destitute of good qualities,[3] which, according to the commentator Medhātithi, include education, courage, good personal appearance, liking for the girl and a number of other good qualities. The rules enjoining the marriage of girls before puberty have till very recently been strictly observed by the Brahmins and by such members of the other twice-born classes as have imitated the customs of the Brahmins. Child-marriage is not common among the Śūdras. Quite recently there has been a tendency even among the

[1] *Manu*, IX, 90.
[2] *Ibid.*, IX, 91.
[3] *Ibid.*, IX, 89.

Brahmins, and especially among the educated classes, in favour of post-puberty marriages. The desire to give an education to their girls and secure educated husbands with prospects of decent employment, the growth of the mercenary spirit of demanding a price for the bridegroom in proportion to his educational qualifications and worldly means or prospects, the difficulty of providing the bridegroom-price at competitive rates and the gradual, though tardy, recognition of the claim of girls to be consulted in the choice of their husbands are among the circumstances which are bringing about a change of opinion in Hindu society. There are numerous instances now of post-puberty marriages, though the attainment of puberty is not always avowed. The recent legislation in restraint of child-marriages associated with the name of Mr. Sarda is not too much in advance of the change of sentiment taking place among the communities affected by it.

The marriage of children and the performance of betrothal by the parents was not unknown at one time even in European countries. The legal age of marriage in England was only 14 for boys and 12 for girls, till it was raised to 16 for both in 1929.

The Hindu law-givers generally contemplated a considerable difference in years between the bridegroom and the bride and required that the bride should be younger in age than the bridegroom. This rule is in accord with the generally accepted notions of propriety and has been largely followed. The requirement of Manu that a man aged thirty years should marry a maiden of twelve or a man of twenty-four should marry a girl of eight years of age[1] was probably based upon the necessity for his completing his course of education. But it may be safely presumed that it was not considered practicable even in his time. The disparity in age between the husband and the wife recommended by Manu is far too great for a happy wedded life and has not generally commended itself to the people. There are several communities among whom the injunction as to the wife being younger than the husband has not been strictly observed. Injunctions as to the relative ages of the husband and wife are only of a recommendatory character.

In almost all societies marriages within certain degrees of kinship are prohibited for a variety of reasons. The restrictions are largely due to the custom of exogamy and eugenic considerations. It is doubtful whether the circle of prohibited degrees has been so large in any community in the world as among the Hindus. The number of prohibited degrees is variously laid down by the different Smṛti writers. According to Manu and some other Smṛtikāras, seven degrees on the father's side and seven degrees on the mother's side are prohibited.[2] Yājñavalkya prohibits seven degrees on the father's side and five on the mother's side.[3] Another sage, Paiṭhīnasi, lays down five degrees on the father's side and three on the mother's.[4] The number of girls who would be

[1] *Manu*, IX, 94.
[2] *Ibid*., III, 5.
[3] *Yājñavalkya*, I, 53.
[4] Referred to in *Mitākṣarā*, I, 53.

ineligible for marriage owing to their Sapiṇḍa relationship with the bridegroom either through the father or the mother has been calculated by Mr. Mandlik to be 2121.[1] This calculation was made on the assumption that the bridegroom was going to be married for the first time and that each married couple in the pedigree had one son and one daughter. The number would have to be greatly increased, if the calculation included relations through the step-mother or through adoption. In practice, however, these rules have not been strictly observed. The ancient law-givers themselves recognised the validity of local exceptions in different parts of India. They make mention of the practice in southern India of marrying the daughter of a paternal aunt or a maternal uncle.[2] Among some communities in southern India, as for instance among the Komuṭis or Vaiśyas and certain sections of Telugu and Mahārāṣṭra Brahmins, the even more objectionable marriage of a sister's daughter has been recognised. So many customs contrary to the Smṛti rules have grown up on the subject that it would be unsafe to lay down without numerous qualifications that a marriage which contravened the degrees of prohibited relationship laid down by the Śāstras would be invalid on that ground.[3] The language used by Manu and Yājñavalkya clearly indicates that the rules are only of a recommendatory character. In what cases a

[1] *Vyavahāra-mayūkha*, pp. 350-352.

[2] *Bodhāyana*, I, i, 2, 3.

[3] See G. C. Sarkar: *Hindu Law* (7th edition), pp. 102, 103, 143, 144.

violation of the rules of prohibited degrees would be regarded as of an incestuous character and shocking to the community concerned, it would be equally difficult to lay down in general rules.

Over and above the rules of prohibited degrees there is another rule which requires that the parties to the marriage should not have the same Gotra or Pravara. The distinction between Gotra and Pravara is not very easy to define. Both the words indicate descent through certain ancestral Ṛṣis who lived thousands of years ago. The memory of this descent is kept up by the members of the twice-born classes by the repetition of the names of the ancestral Ṛṣis during their prayers and on occasions of ceremonial salutation. It can be easily imagined that this principle of exclusion would render ineligible many persons with whom there could be no conceivable bond of relationship by way of blood. One of the parties to a marriage may belong to a family domiciled for centuries in one province of India and the other party may belong to a family similarly domiciled in a different province. It is an illustration of the tendency to apply fictions with a vengeance. Though the rule is even more sweeping and unreasonable than the rule of prohibited degrees, the law-givers ancient and modern have not hesitated to lay down that identity of Gotra between the parties to a marriage renders it invalid. Bodhāyana laid down that if a man unwittingly married a woman of the same Gotra, he should maintain her like a mother.[1] The hold that this prohibition has acquired over the minds even of educated persons is remarkable. Bridegrooms who are otherwise perfectly eligible have often to be ruled out on this ground, and the rule adds to the difficulty of securing suitable husbands for daughters.

The lawfulness of the re-marriage of widows gave rise to a raging controversy in the last century, but the question has been set at rest by legislation. Though the legality of such marriages is not a live issue at the present time, social opinion has been very slow to react in favour of the recognition of such marriages. The prohibition of widow-marriages had its origin in the ideals of asceticism enforced upon widows by a system of man-made laws which did not recognise the principle of equality between the sexes. It is interesting to note that in the *Arthaśāstra* of Kauṭilya which is believed to have been composed about 300 B.C. according to Mr. K. P. Jayaswal and Mr. P. V. Kane and about 300 A.D. according to Prof. A. B. Keith and Dr. J. Jolly, the re-marriage of widows is distinctly recognised and provision is made for her returning to the family of her former husband the property which she had received from him. The re-marriage of a widow was strongly reprobated by Manu as improper. But some of the later Smṛti-writers like Nārada took a more generous view and recognised the right of a widow to marry

[1] *Bọdhāyana*, II, i, 1, 37.

a second husband.[1] That the disapproval did not amount to a declaration of the invalidity of the marriage may be inferred from the text of Yājña-valkya which defines a Punarbhū as a widow who has again undergone the sacrament of marriage, whether her first marriage had been consummated or not by her former husband.[2] Even Manu who has most strongly condemned the re-marriage of widows and described the issue of re-married widows of the twice-born classes as the basest of Dvijas, still considered that they continued to be Dvijas.[3] But Manu's category of the basest Dvijas would include many persons who would be regarded by modern public opinion as perfectly respectable, *e.g.*, Brahmins who receive salaries for teaching or have been taught by salaried teachers or by Śūdras, physicians and those who have crossed the seas.[4] Owing to the growing ascendancy of the ascetic ideal of life for widows, the practice of re-marriage fell into disrepute and at the time of Alberuni's visit to India (*Circa* 1030 A.D.) the re-marriage of widows was prohibited by custom.

Marriage is regarded as a sacrament by the Hindu law-givers. It is also generally supposed to be indissoluble. The text of Parāśara which permits the re-marriage of women clearly contemplates the dissolution of marriage otherwise than by death. The four other cases in which he holds

[1] *Nārada*, XIII, 97; *Vasiṣṭha*, XVII, 20.

[2] *Yājñavalkya*, I, 67.
[3] *Manu*, III, 155.

[4] *Ibid.*, III, 152, 156, 158.
5

that a wife is entitled to re-marry are the disappearance of the husband, his renunciation of the world, his impotency and his expulsion from caste.[1] Where the husband had disappeared, the wife was required to wait for a longer or shorter period according as she had issue or none. These periods varied according to the caste of the wife. Nārada laid down a period of eight and four years respectively for a Brahmin wife, six and three years for a Kṣattriya wife and four and two years for a Vaiśya wife. No definite period was prescribed for a Śudra wife. Twice the above period was ordained when the absent husband was alive and tidings were received of him.[2] The *Arthaśāstra* of Kauṭilya also declares the right of a wife to marry another husband under certain circumstances. "If a husband is absent abroad, undertaking to return after a short period, the wife is bound to wait for a year after the expiry of the period, if she has not given birth to children. If she has had children, she is bound to wait twice as long. If the wife is a virgin, she is bound to wait only from five to ten months according to the circumstances of the case. She may then apply to the judge to dissolve the marriage and may then marry as she likes. If a man is absent for a longer period or becomes a Saṁnyāsin or dies, his wife must wait for seven months. If she has had children, she must wait for a year."[3] It is probable that the

[1] *Parāśara*, IV, 30. See also *Nārada*, XII, 97.
[2] *Nārada*, XII, 98-100.
[3] *Arthaśāstra* (Mysore edition), p. 158-159.

code of Kauṭilya stated the law actually in force and administered by the courts. The same causes which led to the prohibition of widow-marriage by custom operated even more strongly towards the prohibition of dissolution of marriage on the grounds mentioned by the Smṛti-writers referred to above.

While the general Hindu law as enforced by custom set its face against the dissolution of marriage, it has not been opposed to supersession of the wife by the husband. The grounds on which a wife might be superseded by the husband are various and interesting. According to Āpastamba, if one has a wife who is willing and able to perform her share of the religious duties and who bears sons, he should not take a second.[1] "A wife who drinks spirituous liquor, is of bad conduct, rebellious, diseased, mischievous or wasteful may at any time be superseded by another wife. A barren wife may be superseded in the eighth year; she whose children all die, in the tenth; she who bears only daughters, in the eleventh; she who is quarrelsome, without delay. But a sick wife who is kind to her husband and virtuous in her conduct may be superseded only with her own consent and must never be disgraced. A wife who, being superseded, in anger departs from her husband's house, must either be instantly confined or cast off in the presence of the family."[2] The later law-givers too lay down the husband's right of supersession in similar

[1] *Āpastamba*, II, v, 11, 12.
[2] *Manu*, IX, 80-83.

terms.[1] Although superseded, the wife had certain rights against the husband. "One who abandons an obedient, dexterous and sweet-speaking wife who has borne sons should be compelled to give her a third of his property, and if poor, he should be ordered to maintain her."[2] The theoretical right of a Hindu husband to supersede the wife or to take a plurality of wives is but rarely exercised. The practice has been far more considerate to the wife than the strict rule of the law. It was observed by the Abbe Dubois that even among persons of high rank among whom polygyny was tolerated, it was looked upon as an infraction of law and custom, in fact an abuse.[3] At the present time the taking of a second wife without just cause is looked upon by society with feelings of disapproval.

Inter-marriage between the main castes was recognised and permitted by the earlier law-givers, provided the husband belonged to a higher caste than the wife. While wives of the same caste were recommended by preference for the first marriage of the twice-born, they were also allowed to marry women from any of the lower castes.[4] The Sūtra-writers are generally of this view.[5] Manu refers to the rule that a Brahmin could take a wife from any of the three castes below him, a Kṣattriya could take

[1] See *Yājñavalkya*, I, 73.

[2] *Ibid.*, I, 76.

[3] *Hindu Manners, Customs and Ceremonies* (3rd edition), p. 207.

[4] *Manu*, III, 12-13.

[5] *Bodhāyana*, I, viii, 16, 1-5; *Gautama*, IV, 16.

a wife from any of the two lower castes and a Vaiśya could take a wife from the Śūdra caste,[1] but he expresses his own reprobation of the marriage of a Brahmin or a Kṣattriya with a Śūdra woman.[2] "Twice-born men who in their folly wed wives of the Śūdra caste soon degrade their families and their children to the state of Śūdras."[3] According to Yājñavalkya, a Brahmin could take wives only from the first three castes, a Kṣattriya from the second and third and a Vaiśya from the third, *i.e.*, from his own caste.[4] The marriage of a woman of a higher caste with a man of a lower caste was severely condemned by all the Smṛti-writers. Provision was made by the law-givers for the allotment of shares to sons by wives of different castes, a higher share being assigned to the son by the wife of a superior caste. The offspring of these mixed marriages were held to belong to an intermediate caste between that of the father and the mother and different names were assigned to the castes of the offspring of the various forms of mixed marriages. Inter-marriages of the Anuloma form (*i.e.*, of a woman with a man of higher caste) are mentioned without disapproval by the *Dāyabhāga, Smṛticandrikā, Vīramitrodaya* and other digests. The latest commentators on the Hindu law like Kamalākara and Raghunandana prohibited inter-marriages between the four castes. It is most probable that the opinion expressed by the latest com-

[1] *Manu*, III, 13.
[2] *Ibid.*, III, 14.
[3] *Ibid.*, III, 15.
[4] *Yājñavalkya*, I, 57.

mentators reflected the popular opinion at the time when they wrote their treatises. Inter-marriages between the different main castes generally fell out of use and were disapproved by public opinion. The growing rigidity of caste distinctions must have led to the desuetude of inter-marriages. The rule of prohibition which was inferred from the disappearance of inter-marriages used to be strictly enforced by the courts in British India. Quite recently, however, there has been a disposition on the part of some of the High Courts in British India to reconsider the soundness of these decisions and it has been held by the High Court of Bombay[1] that Anuloma marriages are valid. The strong feeling of repugnance entertained towards Pratiloma marriages (*i.e.,* of women with men of lower caste) is not difficult to understand, if we remember the ethical, social and occupational differences which underlie the organisation of Hindu society into four castes and the intense feeling of disapproval with which the marriage of a white woman to a coloured man is regarded in several parts of South Africa and America.

Sonship.

In no chapter of the Hindu law is the progress of moral ideals more unmistakable than in the one which deals with sonship. Nor is there any which better exposes the fallacy of the theory which regards the Kaliyuga as the age of corruption and the past ages as ages of perfection. The necessity

[1] *Bai Gulab* v. *Jiwanlal,* I.L.R. 46 Bom. 871.

for male offspring was strongly felt in all primitive societies for the protection of the aged, the weak and the infirm members of the family for the defence of the community against external aggression and for the purpose of making wars of conquest against weaker communities. The claims of man to the management and ownership of the family property and the system of inheritance in the male line naturally grew up out of early social conditions. Property and inheritance became linked with the system of funeral offerings on the principle enunciated by Manu that he who takes the inheritance must make the funeral offerings. The practice of worship of the spirits of deceased ancestors and the necessity of periodical ceremonies for the benefit of their manes intensified the longing for male issue, to save the ancestors from the torments of hell. The ancient Hindu was anxious to beget sons, and if he did not beget any himself, was anxious to procure a son by some means or other. Having regard to the looseness of the marriage tie in primitive times and the ancient theory that the wife was the chattel of the husband, sons begotten upon the wife by strangers were regarded as belonging to the husband. If we remember that the *patria potestas* which was a characteristic feature of the patriarchal form of society included absolute powers of disposition over the persons of children, we shall have no difficulty in understanding how the list of subsidiary sons came to be augmented by the inclusion of sons given, sold or abandoned by their parents.

Twelve different kinds of sons were recognised by the ancient law. The lists as given by the different Smṛti-writers are not altogether the same. Some kinds of sons mentioned by some Smṛti-writers are omitted by others who include other kinds of sons. According to some writers the twelve sons are divided into two groups, the first six in the order of enumeration being regarded as heirs, while the latter six are regarded as being entitled only to a fractional share for maintenance. According to other writers, all the classes of sons mentioned in the list are heirs, each succeeding class being entitled to inherit on failure of the former. The twelve different kinds of sons said to have been recognised by the first or Svāyambhuva Manu are Aurasa, Kṣetraja, Datta, Kṛtrima, Gūḍhaja, Apaviddha, Kānīna, Sahoḍhaja, Krīta, Paunarbhava, Svayaṁ-datta and Śaudra.[1] It is not necessary to go into details with regard to the order in which these different classes of sons are enumerated by the various Smṛti-writers. The curious may be referred to the table prepared by Mr. J. D. Mayne in his work on Hindu law.[2] It is sufficient here to observe that the Kṣetraja son, *i.e.*, son begotten on the wife by a stranger, occupies a very high place in the list according to the majority of the Smṛtis and that the Datta or adopted son is included among the first six classes (who are alone, according to some, entitled to inherit) by five only out of the fourteen authorities referred to by Mr. Mayne.

[1] *Manu*, IX, 159-160.

[2] *Hindu Law and Usage* (7th edition), p. 82.

The theory underlying the status of the Kṣetraja son is that the wife is regarded as the property of the husband and that if a stranger sows in another's field, the fruit belongs to the owner of the land. The low position assigned to the Datta or son given (*i.e.*, adopted) was probably due to the growth of the sentiment against the gift of a son in the exercise of the *patria potestas*. Āpastamba considered it sinful to make a gift or sale of a son.[1] This view is confirmed by the fact that according to the definition given by Manu, a Datta is a son whom his father or mother may give in distress.[2] The word 'distress' is interpreted by some commentators to mean 'in the absence of issue to the receiver of the son'. This does not seem to me to be the grammatical construction. The distress contemplated by the text is the distress of the givers alone who are referred to and not the spiritual distress of the taker from want of male issue, and this construction is supported by Āpastamba's prohibition of the gift of a son. All these various classes of subsidiary sons except the given or adopted son have now become obsolete.

Property.

The history of the institution of family exhibits the changes which took place from time to time in the conception of ownership. As in other countries in the world, the family was originally of the patriarchal type and the joint family was evolved

[1] *Āpastamba*, II, vi, 13, 11.
[2] *Manu*, IX, 168.

from it. The transition from the patriarchal to the joint family arose at the death of the common ancestor or patriarch of the family. During his lifetime the patriarch or head of the family exercised despotic authority over the property and the persons of the members of his family. The powers of the Hindu father or ancestor were practically the same as those included in the *patria potestas* of the Roman law. On the death of the father the eldest son succeeded to his position as head of the family; but as pointed out by Mr. Mayne, his position as head of the family was the result of a delegated authority from his brothers. The eldest brother, however, did not always succeed to this position, for he might be superseded by a more capable younger brother. The extent of the authority possessed by the manager of a joint family composed of collaterals was necessarily different from that of the despotic patriarch. As regards his collaterals, he was merely a manager whose position depended upon their consent. He was restricted in his dealings with the property as against the collateral members of the family and in course of time these restrictions were extended even as against his own descendants. We find in the Smṛtis texts relating to different stages in the evolution of the family. But as usual they are all treated by the law-givers and commentators as equally applicable to all the stages in the growth of the family, and the difficulties in reconciling the texts offer a wide field for the exercise of the ingenuity of the jurists. A text of Manu declares that a wife, a son and a slave have no property and that the wealth which they earn is acquired for him to whom they belong.[1] Obviously this refers to the patriarchal stage. During this stage the whole of the property was owned by the father and all acquisitions made by the members of the family were made for him. It was only after the break-up of the patriarchal family and the rise of the joint family that separate property and self-acquisitions became possible. In the earlier stages of society, before the growth of industry and commerce, the opportunities for the acquisition of separate property were few. The doctrine of self-acquired property in Hindu law was of slow growth and, as pointed out by Mr. Mayne, sprang from a desire to reconcile the conflicting interests of the acquirer and the joint family of which he was a member. Manu declares that what a brother has acquired by his labour without using the patrimony cannot be shared without his consent, for it was acquired by his own exertion.[2] If the gains of learning were earned by means of instruction imparted at the expense of the family, Kātyāyana and Bṛhaspati refuse to recognise the exclusive right of the acquirer.[3] Even where the self-acquisition of a member was recognised, the only benefit obtained by the acquirer was the right to retain a double or extra share of his acquisitions.[4] As

[1] *Manu*, VIII, 416.
[2] *Ibid.*, IX, 208.
[3] *Kātyayanasmṛti* on *Vyavahāra* (edited by P. V. Kane, 1933), verse 874.
[4] *Vasiṣṭha*, XVII, 51.

regards the right of disposition of the acquirer over his self-acquisition, the *Mitākṣarā* quoted with approval a text declaring that though immovables or bipeds have been acquired by a man himself, a gift or sale of them should not be made without convening all the sons.[1] It was at one time doubtful whether in the *Mitākṣarā* school a father had absolute control over his self-acquired immovable property. But it is now settled that there is no distinction as to the acquirer's powers of alienation between movable and immovable property.

The right to demand partition of the family property was only developed by a very gradual process. In the earlier period of Hindu law a son had no right to demand partition from his father. Manu spoke of a division only after the death of the father and expressly said that the brothers had no power over the property while the parents lived.[2] Bodhāyana, Gautama and other writers declared the consent of the father to be indispensable for a partition of ancestral property.[3] The *Mitākṣarā* explained away the text of Manu as referring to the self-acquired property of the father and laid down that the son had a right to demand partition of the ancestral estate.[4] The same texts upon which the *Mitākṣarā* came to the conclusion that the son had a right to demand partition were relied

1 *Mitākṣarā*, II, 113. (Introduction to Dāyavibhāgaprakaraṇa).
2 *Manu*, IX, 104.
3 *Bodhāyana*, II, ii, 3, 8; *Gautama*, XXVIII, 2.
4 *Mitākṣarā*, II, 121.

upon by the *Dāyabhāga* to support the opposite conclusion that the sons had no right to compel a partition during the father's lifetime and that the sons' right to the father's property arose only on the latter's death.

A wife has no right to demand a partition of the property from her husband. If he made a partition of the family property, dividing it in equal shares among his sons, his wives to whom no peculium (Strīdhana) has been given by him or his father were entitled, according to the *Mitākṣarā,* to shares equal to that of the sons. But if any Strīdhana had been given to them by him or his father, they were entitled to half the share of a son.[1] But if after the death of their husband the sons entered into a partition, they were entitled to shares equal to that of a son, though they could not claim a partition at their own instance. Under the *Dāyabhāga* a sonless step-mother is not entitled to a share on partition between the step-sons. In southern India the practice of allotting a share on partition to wives, widows or mothers has long since become obsolete. According to the Benares law, not only mothers, but also childless wives were entitled to a share when partition took place at the instance of sons or male members.

Liability for ancestor's debts.

According to the Hindu law, the sons and grandsons were under a religious obligation to pay the debts of their father or grandfather, even if

[1] *Mitākṣarā,* II, 115.

they inherited no ancestral property. There was a distinction, however, between the sons and the grandsons, for while the former were bound to pay the father's debt with interest, the latter were only bound to pay the debt of the grandfather without interest. But this moral and religious obligation did not extend to debts of an illegal or immoral character. Under the law as now administered by the courts in all provinces except Bombay, the liability to pay the ancestor's debt is only enforced to the extent of the assets inherited from him.[1]

Maintenance.

Apart from the obligation to maintain all the members of the family who were entitled to claim a share, the Hindu law imposed an obligation to maintain other members who were not entitled to a share. In some cases the obligation was based upon the possession of property and in other cases it was unconditional and absolute. It is laid down in the *Mitākṣarā* that where there may be no property, but what has been self-acquired, the only persons whose maintenance out of such property is imperative are aged parents, wife and minor children.[2]

Illegitimate sons, except in the cases in which they are entitled as heirs, and concubines whose connection was of a permanent nature are entitled to maintenance. There is a difference of opinion

[1] J. D. Mayne: *Hindu Law and Usage* (7th edition), p. 390.
[2] *Ibid.*, p. 605.

between the Bengal school and the others as to whether the right of maintenance continues after the illegitimate son attains majority. It has now been held by the Privy Council that the illegitimate son is entitled to claim maintenance for life from the surviving coparceners of his father out of the joint family property which has passed to them.[1] The widows of the members of the family are of course entitled, so long as they lead a virtuous life, to maintenance. The widow of a son has no legal claim to maintenance against the separate or self-acquired property of her father-in-law, but the courts have held that the father-in-law is under a moral obligation to support her and that this moral obligation is converted into a legal obligation in the hands of his heirs.

Inheritance.

The ancient writers on Hindu law were unfavourable to the recognition of women's rights of inheritance.[2] A woman has no right to independence; the father protects her in her childhood, the husband in her youth and the son in her old age.[3] Bodhāyana and Vasiṣṭha mention no females in their list of heirs and the former expressly states on the authority of a text in the Veda that women

[1] Vellaiyappa Chetti *vs.* Natarajan, I.L.R. 55 M. 1 (P.C.).

[2] The Hindu law was not singular in this respect. The patriarchal system was generally unfavourable to the recognition of the rights of women to inheritance and independence. This was a feature of the law both in the East and in the West not merely in antiquity, but even in modern times. (*Cf.* E. Westermarck: *The Origin and Development of the Moral Ideas*, Vol. II, pp. 47, 48, 55.)

[3] *Bodhāyana*, II, ii, 3, 45; *Manu*, IX, 3.

have no right to inherit.[1] Their right to inheritance was a matter of slow growth. Manu recognises the right of a mother to inherit to a son who dies without issue. If the mother is dead, the paternal grandmother is entitled to take the estate. Some of the commentators explain that the place of the paternal grandmother in the scheme of succession is not immediately after the mother, but on failure of certain other relations also.[2] The right of the widow of a person dying without sons to succeed to his property was recognised later than that of other women who now take after her. The earlier writers like Manu, Āpastamba, and Vasiṣṭha did not recognise her right as heir, though they acknowledged that of the daughter and mother. The widow, however, can succeed as such only to the property of her husband.[3] Except in Bombay, no fresh right can accrue to her as a widow in consequence of the subsequent death of someone to whom her husband would have been heir if he had lived. The general principle adopted by the Bengal, Benares and Mithilā schools is that no female can inherit to a male unless she is expressly named as an heir in the texts. In Bombay the widows of Gotraja Sapiṇḍas are brought in as heirs, but the female Sapiṇḍā in any line cannot exclude any male belonging to that line. As Mr. Mayne points out, this is one of those cases in which usages which sprang up without any refer-

[1] *Bodhāyana*, II, ii, 3, 46.

[2] *Manu*, IX, 217 and commentaries.

[3] J. D. Mayne: *Hindu Law and Usage* (7th edition), p. 794.

ence to the Sanskrit law-books are now supported by torturing those books so as to draw from them conclusions of which their authors had no idea.[1] The sister's right of succession has been admitted in Bombay on the ground that though she has passed by marriage to another family, she is a Gotraja Sapiṇḍā in the sense that she was born in the family. The sister and certain other female heirs were recognised in Madras as entitled to succeed on failure of all male cognates. The decision of the Madras High Court in favour of the admission of the sister was vigorously attacked by Mr. Mayne and shown to be inconsistent with the principles by which succession is regulated in southern India. By recent legislation[2] applicable to all provinces following the *Mitākṣarā*, a son's daughter, a sister and a sister's son have been allowed to inherit in this order next after a father's father and before a father's brother. The rights of Hindu women to a share in the family property, to inheritance, to the control and disposition of their property and to maintenance have been greatly enlarged by recent legislation in the enlightened State of Mysore.[3]

As between the parents, the mother is considered by the *Mitākṣarā* to be a nearer heir than the father on the ground of a greater corporeal connection between the mother and child.[4] In Bengal the father takes before the mother upon the prin-

[1] J. D. Mayne: *Hindu Law and Usage* (7th edition), p. 717; 5 Bom. 110.

[2] Act II of 1929.

[3] Regulation X of 1933.

[4] *Mitākṣarā*, II, 135.

ciple of religious efficacy adopted by the *Dāyabhāga* and on the text of *Viṣṇu*.[1]

Strīdhana.

The right of a woman to hold separate property of her own was recognised in the Hindu law long before it was admitted in European countries.[2] Presents given to a woman at her marriage by her own relations or her husband and what she received after marriage from her husband and his family were treated as her peculium. Property received by a maiden in the shape of ornaments or other presents from her own family or from her affianced

[1] *Viṣṇu*, XVII, 7.

[2] *See* Banerji: *Marriage and Stridhan*. *Cf.* E. Westermarck: *The Origin and Development of the Moral Ideas*, Vol. II, pp. 30-31. "In Rome a marriage with *conventio in manum*, which was the regular form of marriage in early times, gave the husband a right to all the property which the wife had when she married, and entitled him to all she might acquire afterwards whether by gift or by her own labour. Later on, marriage without *manus* became the ordinary Roman marriage, and this, together with the downfall of the ancient *patria potestas*, led to the result that finally all the wife's property was practically under her own control, save when a part of it had been converted by settlement into a fund for contributing to the expenses of the conjugal household. But as we have noticed in another place, the new religion was not favourable to the remarkable liberty granted to married women during the pagan Empire; and the combined influence of Teutonic custom and Canon law led to those proprietary incapacities of wives which up to quite recent times have disfigured the law-books of Christian Europe. In England, before 1857, even a man who had abandoned his wife and left her unaided to support his family might at any time return to appropriate her earnings and to sell everything she had acquired, and he might again and again desert her and again and again repeat the process of spoliation. In 1870 a law was passed securing to women the legal control of their own earnings, but all other female property with some insignificant exceptions, was left absolutely unprotected. And it was not until the Married Women's Property Act of 1882 that a full right to their own property was given to English wives."

bridegroom was regarded as her own property. The *Mitākṣarā* included under the term Strīdhana all property lawfully obtained by a woman. But she did not possess the same powers of disposition over all kinds of property belonging to her. With regard to some kinds of property, she could dispose of them absolutely at her own pleasure and could not be controlled by her husband in her dealings with them. But the husband could take the property in case of extreme distress, as in a famine, or for some indispensable duty, or during illness, or if a creditor put him in prison.[1] Wealth earned by a woman by mechanical arts was subject to the husband's control, according to Kātyāyana.[2]

Illegitimate son's right to inherit.

Illegitimate sons in the three higher castes are not heirs at all, but are only entitled to maintenance from the estate of their father. The illegitimate son of a Śūdra, however, may inherit under certain circumstances either jointly or solely. His right is based upon the texts of Manu and Yājñavalkya. Yājñavalkya laid down that even a son begotten by a Śūdra on a Dāsī may take a share by the father's choice. But if the father be dead, the brothers should make him partaker of a moiety of a share; and one who has no brothers may inherit the whole property in default of daughter's sons.[3] It has now been settled by judicial decisions that

[1] *Yājñavalkya*, II, 147.
[2] *Kātyāyana-smṛti* on *Vyavahāra* (edited by P. V. Kane, 1933), verse 904.
[3] *Yājñavalkya*, II, 133-134.

the mother of the illegitimate son of a Śūdra need not be a slave and that 'Dāsī' means only an unmarried woman kept as a continuous concubine and that the connection with her must not have been adulterous or unlawful.

Exclusion from inheritance.

The Hindu law-givers excluded persons from inheritance on a variety of grounds. Apart from the disqualification originally imposed upon women by reason of their sex, serious mental, physical, moral or religious defects were considered to disqualify even males from inheritance. The main grounds of exclusion were those mentioned by Manu and Yājñavalkya, *viz.*, impotence, degradation from caste, congenital blindness or deafness, insanity, idiocy, dumbness, deficiency of a sense or limb and affliction with an incurable disease[1] which was subsequently limited to the worst forms of leprosy. One main reason for the disqualification of these persons was their incompetency for the performance of sacrifices and other religious ceremonies. According to Kātyāyana, wealth was made for sacrifices and it should therefore be appropriated to fit and virtuous persons and not to women and ignorant or irreligious men.[2] A legislator may take the view that wealth should devolve upon those who are most in need of it by reason of their necessitous condition or upon those who are competent to make a proper use of it. The

[1] *Manu*, IX, 201; *Yājñavalkya*, II, 140.

[2] J. C. Ghose: *The Principles of Hindu Law*, p. 198.

Hindu law-givers seem to have taken the view that merit rather than need should be the ground of inheritance. Some of the ancient writers excluded persons who were addicted to vice, or who were hypocrites or impostors or who were wanting in sacred knowledge, courage, industry, devotion or liberality, or failed to observe immemorial good customs. These rules furnish an illustration of the tendency of the Brahmin law-givers to confound the provinces of law and morality. As pointed out by Mr. Mayne, such a system could never have been practically enforced and the parallel theory of expiation rendered it profitable to the priestly class and endurable by the rest of the community. This is the general tendency of ecclesiastical laws in other parts of the world. The only grounds of disqualification recognised by the courts in British India were those mentioned by Yājña-valkya. The disability caused by change of religion and degradation from caste was removed by the Caste Disabilities Removal Act.[1] In cases not governed by the Bengal School of Hindu Law the disabilities arising from disease, deformity, or physical or mental defect not amounting to congenital lunacy or idiocy have now been abolished by recent legislation.[2]

[1] Act XXI of 1850.
[2] Act XII of 1928.

CHAPTER III.

WOMAN

The estimation in which woman is held, the status occupied by her in society and the treatment accorded to her have been justly regarded as marks of the degree of civilisation and culture attained in any country. Our moral ideals regarding women have been too often conceived in a narrow sense as concerned with the department of what has been called sexual morality and with the obligations of chastity and marital fidelity. The ideals of womanhood include not merely the relations of husband and wife or mother and children or the other intimate relationships of family life, but the recognition accorded to her personality, the notions we form about her capacity, her character, her claim to equality, independence and freedom for development, her rights to personal liberty, to the ownership and control of property, to the choice of her vocation and to her rights as well as duties as a member of society. Our notions in all these matters have been largely moulded by the conditions of the age and the country, by our outlook on the problems of life, by our religious beliefs, by the influence of traditions and by intellectual progress and the growth of rationalism. Ideals formed in particular conditions of society do not hold good when the conditions have undergone a radical change. In the unsettled conditions through which many societies have passed and in times when the need for defence against external enemies was imperative, the special qualities and virtues of the weaker sex would have less scope for exercise and women would be relegated to a subordinate position to men. The partiarchal type of society which at one time prevailed in India as well as in other countries was based upon the predominance of the male sex and has deeply affected the structure of the family and the ownership and inheritance of property. The growing recognition of the rights of individual members of joint families to property acquired by their own exertions and the disintegration of the joint family system favoured the growth of women's rights of inheritance. The change from militant to peaceful conditions of society and from agricultural to industrial and commercial occupations, the concentration of population in towns with their variety of occupations and communities, the looseness of ties between the different sections of the urban population and the growth of competitive conditions of life have all profoundly influenced our social ideals including our ideals of womanhood.

The ideals of womanhood of which we have evidence in the Vedic age were not the same as those which obtained in the age of the epics and the earlier Smṛtis. Nor were these latter the same as those which have been preserved to us in the classical age of Sanskrit literature. There have been changes in the position of women in society from age to age. In the Vedic age women were not denied the advantages of education in sacred literature. They were not considered incompetent to study the Vedas or the Dharma Śāstras or the systems of philosophy then in existence. Some of the hymns of the Ṛg Veda were composed by women. They could be invested with the sacred thread and could perform the Sandhyā prayers including the repetition of the Sāvitrī. After finishing their course of education they could either enter upon married life or devote themselves to religious and metaphysical studies, just like men. The Upaniṣads contain evidence of learned women taking part in philosophical discussions in public assemblies. As married women, they took part in the sacrifices performed by their husbands and the term 'Patnī' which is applied to a wife indicates this participation.

Women were not married before puberty. The Mantras prescribed during the marriage ceremonies afford the clearest evidence that the parties to the marriage were of competent age and that the marriage was immediately followed by cohabitation. The parties to the marriage seem to have had a voice in the selection of their partners. By her marriage a wife obtained a position of honour in the house of her husband. She was the mistress of her husband's house, exercising authority over her father-in-law, her husband's brothers and his unmarried sisters. This is reconcilable with the patriarchal theory only on the supposition that the eldest son of a family has become its head owing to the decrepitude of his parents. Where the husband died without issue, his widow was allowed to raise up male issue to him by marriage with the husband's brother. While it is probable that the vast majority of women preferred a married life, some of them, either by choice or by necessity, led a life of celibacy. An old spinster who remained without finding a husband was called अमाजुर् or पितृषद्. Women could freely appear in public and were not required to observe seclusion.

If in these respects the position of women in Vedic times was superior to that of women in later times, it was no better in regard to rights to property and inheritance. This is of course quite consistent with the patriarchal structure of society and the theory of perpetual tutelage which has been applied to women in the earlier stages of history in all civilised communities. In ancient Greece 'at no time of her life could a woman be without a guardian. If her father was not alive, it would be her nearest male relative, and this person remained her guardian even when she was married. After her husband's death her son was her guardian.'[1] So in India during the lifetime of the father the daughter was dependent on him and on his death she was supported and protected by her brothers. Brotherless maidens were exposed to danger and this is the reason for the injunction that a maiden with brothers was to be preferred for marriage. During the Smṛti period when society had settled into orderly conditions, a dif-

[1] T. G. Tucker: *Life in Ancient Athens*, p. 52.

ferent reason was assigned for the disapproval of the marriage of brotherless girls. According to Manu, the danger in this case was that the daughter might be a Putrikā or appointed daughter whose son by virtue of the appointment would become the son of his grandfather[1] by a legal fiction or by convention.

Polygyny was being replaced in the Ṛg Vedic period by monogamy. Unchastity on the part of the wife was strongly condemned and adultery was severely punished.

During the period of the Sūtra-writers the position of women underwent serious deterioration in many respects, just as there was degradation in the position of the Athenian wife after the days of Homer.[2] The position of the Hindu wife during the epic period and even till quite recently was very similar to that of the Roman wife in the age of Cicero.[3] Women were debarred from the study of

[1] *Manu*, III, 11.

[2] "It is a great blot on Athenian civilisation that the position of women had retrograded since the days of Homer. Her business now is simply to be the housewife and housemother, to apportion to the slaves their domestic work, to regulate the stores; to weave and superintend the weaving of garments, and to bring up the girls and little boys. She has received no particular education beyond these domestic accomplishments. She may go abroad at festivals and on other recognised occasions, if properly attended, but the best woman, according to the Athenian definition, is she of whom 'least is said for either good or harm'." (T. G. Tucker: *Life in Ancient Athens*, p. 51.)

[3] "No one who studies this ceremonial of Roman marriage, in the light of the ideas which it indicates and reflects, can avoid the conclusion that the position of the married woman must have been one of substantial dignity, calling for and calling out a corresponding type of character. Beyond doubt the position of the Roman

the Vedas and were considered to be unfit to pronounce Vedic Mantras. The marriage ceremony is stated to be the only sacrament for women which could be performed with Vedic Mantras.[1] The reasons assigned for this rule are that women were destitute of a knowledge of the Vedic texts and destitute of strength. Women were debarred from Upanayana or investiture with the sacred thread, and not being initiated, were declared to be unfit for the study of the Vedas. In this respect they were placed in the same position as Śūdras. Protests were not wanting on the part of some of the Smṛti-writers against this degradation of women. Hārīta says that "women of the higher castes are not equal in status to Śūdras. From a Śūdra womb Brāhmaṇas, Kṣattriyas and Vaiśyas cannot be born. Therefore women deserve to have the sacraments performed with Vedic texts."[2] It is difficult to conceive the reasons why women were

materfamilias was a much more dignified one than that of the Greek wife. She was far indeed from being a mere drudge or squaw; she shared with her husband in all the duties of the household, including those of religion, and within the house itself she was practically supreme. She lived in the atrium, and was not shut away in a woman's chamber; she nursed her own children and brought them up; she had entire control of the female slaves who were her maids; she took her meals with her husband, but sitting, not reclining, and abstaining from wine; in all practical matters she was consulted, and only on questions political or intellectual was she expected to be silent. When she went out arrayed in the graceful *stola matronalis*, she was treated with respect, and the passers-by made way for her; but it is characteristic of her position that she did not as a rule leave the house without the knowledge of her husband, or without an escort." (W. Warde Fowler: *Social Life at Rome in the Age of Cicero*, pp. 143-144.)

[1] *Vyāsa*, I, 16.

[2] *Hārīta*, XXI, 20.

prohibited from a study of the Vedas. That Manu took a low view of women's intelligence may be inferred from verse 77 of chapter VIII, where he observes that the understanding of females is apt to waver and that they do not make good witnesses. They were required to obtain a knowledge of duty and morality by a study of the Purāṇas. If the charge of want of understanding were true at all, it would be the necessary result of their being deprived of education. It is an argument very familiar in the mouths of those who are opposed to the emancipation of women. Women were declared by the Smṛti-writers to be unfit for independence and they were to be kept under tutelage during their whole life.

Child-marriages came into vogue in the Smṛti period. The postponement of marriage till after puberty is disapproved by the Sūtrakāras and by the Smṛti-writers. The old marriage ritual, however, which was in terms applicable only to grown-up maidens was still retained without any sense of incongruity. The re-marriage of widows was also recognised by the later Dharma Sūtras and the Smṛti-writers.[1]

Of the eight forms of marriage referred to by Manu and other Smṛti-writers some had become obsolete and merely possessed a historical significance. The Paiśāca form which was strongly condemned had probably become obsolete. The Asura form which consisted in the purchase of the

[1] *Vasiṣṭha*, XVII, 19, 20, 72, 74; *Bodhāyana*, IV, i, 16.

bride on payment of a price to her father was also censured by Manu as amounting to a sale of the girl and therefore immoral. As this form of marriage has continued down to modern times, it may be presumed that it was in use in spite of the moral prohibition. The Rākṣasa form of marriage by capture was pronounced by Manu to be lawful for the members of the warrior caste. Polygyny was sanctioned by Manu, but the first marriage alone was regarded as performed from a sense of religious duty and for religious purposes and the subsequent marriages were regarded as merely the result of natural inclinations. The obligation to conjugal fidelity was laid down in the most emphatic terms. The breach of the obligation, however, was not so serious an offence in the case of the husband as in the case of the wife. Manu says "Let mutual fidelity continue until death. This is the summary of the highest law for husband and wife. Let man and woman united in marriage constantly exert themselves so that even if separated, they may not violate their mutual fidelity."[1] It has been observed by Lecky that "in its oriental or polygamous stage marriage is regarded almost exclusively, in its lowest aspect, as a gratification of the animal passions, while in European marriages the mutual attachment and respect of the contracting parties, the formation of a household, and the long train of domestic feelings and duties that accompany it, have all their distinguished place among the motives of the contract and the lower

[1] *Manu*, IX, 101-102.

element has comparatively little prominence."[1] Whatever may be the correctness of Lecky's observations with regard to marriage in European or other countries, they are not correct as to the Hindu conception of marriage. Marriage has been regarded by the Hindus not as a mere contract, but as a sacrament witnessed by the gods. Marriage is inspired by religious as well as secular motives. In no other system has marriage been more strongly associated with, and prompted by, religious motives. The necessity of periodical offerings to the spirits of the departed ancestors and the desire for the perpetuation of one's lineage have both combined to plant in the mind of the Hindu a strong desire for offspring and especially for sons. The objects intended to be secured by marriage are offspring, the due performance of religious rites, faithful attendance (service), the highest conjugal happiness and heavenly bliss for the ancestors and oneself, and they are all declared to depend on one's wife alone.[2] According to Manu, the man who has not taken a wife has not fully perfected his personality and must be regarded as incomplete and imperfect. His personality is developed and completed only upon the union of three persons, his wife, himself and his offspring. The Vedas and learned Brāhmaṇas have laid down the maxim that the husband and the wife are one in person.[3] Though Manu did not entertain a very high opinion

[1] W. E. H. Lecky: *History of European Morals* (*Library edition*), Vol. II, pp. 294-295.

[2] *Manu*, IX, 28.

[3] *Ibid.*, IX, 45.

of the female intellect, an opinion which has to this day not been abandoned by many thinkers and public men even in the West,[1] he insisted that women should be honoured by their husbands and relations. "Women must be honoured (and adorned) by their fathers, brothers, husbands and brothers-in-law who desire their own welfare. Where women are honoured, there the gods are pleased; but where they are not honoured, no sacred rite yields rewards. Where the female relations live in grief, the family soon wholly perishes; but that family where they are not unhappy, ever prospers. The houses on which female relations, not being duly honoured, pronounce a curse, perish completely as if destroyed by magic. Hence men who seek their own welfare should always honour women on holidays and festivals with gifts of ornaments, clothes and dainty food. In that family where the husband is pleased with his wife and the wife with her husband, happiness would assuredly be lasting."[2] The *Mahābhārata* says that one who desires prosperity must honour and respect women and that a wife who is petted and favoured is the goddess of fortune.[3]

As regards the character of women, contradictory opinions can be found in Manu as in the writings of many a moralist and poet all over the

[1] W. E. H. Lecky remarked that the intellectual inferiority of women to men was as undeniable as their moral superiority over men was unquestionable. (*History of European Morals,* (*Library edition*), Vol. II, pp. 379-380.)

[2] *Manu*, III, 55-60.

[3] *Anuśasanaparva,* 46, 15.

world.[1] No unfavourable inference can be drawn from such passages. Such contradictory opinions are due to the existence in every society of different types of character among women as well as men and the opinions are often the reflection of the temperament and the feelings of those who express them. The opinion of womenkind expressed by a disappointed suitor or an aggrieved husband necessarily differs from that of a successful one or the happy husband. In some passages of his Smṛti Manu expresses the opinion that women are weak, frail and flighty and must be guarded against temptation, but in another passage he says that women cannot be guarded by force and that those women are best protected from temptation who are shielded by their own character. "Women confined in the house under trustworthy and obedient servants are not really guarded, but those who of their own accord keep guard over themselves are well guarded."[2] He points out the habits which bring women to grief and advises husbands to employ them in the collection and expenditure of their wealth, in keeping everything clean and tidy, in the fulfilment of religious duties, in the preparation of their food and in looking after the household utensils and furniture.[3] He evidently thinks that the idleness of women leads to mischief. He declares that between the goddess of fortune who resides in the house and wives who are

[1] *Cf.* E. Westermarck: *The Origin and Development of the Moral Ideas,* Vol. I, pp. 661-663.

[2] *Manu,* IX, 12.

[3] *Ibid.,* IX, 11.

destined to bear children, who secure many blessings, who are worthy of worship and irradiate their dwellings, there is no difference whatsoever.[1]

The theory of *patria potestas* continued to exercise its influence in the Smṛti age also. It was a logical consequence of this theory that the father of the family could administer correction to his wife, a son, a slave, a pupil and a uterine younger brother who have committed faults. But the chastisement had to be moderate and could be administered only with a rope or a split bamboo and only on the back part of the body and not on the head.[2]

Though earlier writers like Bodhāyana declared the incompetency of women for inheritance

[1] *Manu*, IX, 26.

[2] *Cf.* "The laws and public opinion in most countries then sanctioned the corporal chastisement of wives. The amount of this practically depended entirely on the husband's judgment. The English law, that he might use no stick thicker than his thumb, very slightly limited his power, and such as it was, was evaded by some brutes who 'put a rod in pickle', that is, soaked it with salt and vinegar in order to make the wales more painful." (P. Smith: *A History of Modern Culture*, p. 529.)

"The husband also (by the old law) might give his wife moderate correction. For, as he is to answer for her misbehaviour, the law thought it reasonable to entrust him with the power of restraining her, by domestic chastisement, in the same moderation that a man is allowed to correct his apprentices or children." (L. T. Hobhouse: *Morals in Evolution*, Vol. I, p. 225.)

"Women (in England) had acquired personal protection from the wife-beating husband during the 'politer reign of Charles II'." (L. T. Hobhouse: *Morals in Evolution*, Vol. I, p. 228.)

"In an essay on the position of women among the early Christians Principal Donaldson writes, 'In the first three centuries I have not been able to see that Christianity had any favourable effect on the position of women, but, on the contrary, that it tended to lower their character and contract the range of their activity.' " (E. Westermarck: *The Origin and Development of the Moral Ideas*, Vol. I, p. 654.)

on the ground of their deficiency of strength, the text of Manu which lays down the inheritance of the nearest Sapiṇḍās has been interpreted by the commentators as recognising the right of the wife as a Sapiṇḍā.[1] There are also other passages to be found in Manu recognising the capacity of women to hold property.

Yet another deduction from the *patria potestas* was that the right to dispose of her daughter in marriage originally vested in the mother only in default of the father, the grandfather, brother or even Sakulya.[2] The strict application of the principle was rejected in Madras and it was held by the High Court that the object of placing the male relations before the mother was merely to supply that protection and advice which the Hindu system considered to be necessary on account of the dependent condition of women.[3] That dependence has now practically ceased to be enforced by the law.

One important feature of the Hindu religious system remains to be noticed. Unlike Christianity, Hinduism never attached any notion of impurity to sex. Marriage was regarded not as a concession to the weakness of human nature, nor was married life regarded as a morally inferior condition to virginity. No pre-eminence was attached to virginity as distinguished from chastity in the scale of virtues. Nor did any cult of virginity

[1] *Manu,* IX, 187 and commentaries.
[2] *Yājñavalkya,* I, 63; *Nārada,* XII, 20-21.
[3] 4 Madras High Court Reports, 339.

establish itself, as in early Christianity, till later times when Śakti worship came into vogue. Life-long celibacy was permitted, but never enjoined as an ideal. The practice of asceticism in India did not have a degrading effect upon the general conception of sex in religion or in society.[1] Asceticism has been practised in India merely as a temporary method of discipline and self-restraint or as a means to the acquisition of magical powers, and the ascetic ideal has never been exalted at the expense of the ideal of the householder. Numerous are the instances of married persons who attained to the greatest holiness and wisdom and were regarded as sages and saints entitled to the highest reverence. Nearly all the great Ṛṣis or seers were married men and their wives equally with them were looked upon as exemplars of the highest virtue. The fact that anthropomorphic conceptions of the deity in India included both the female and the male elements is an illustration of the absence in the Hindu mind of all notions of impurity about sex.

[1] Ascetic Christianity represented woman as the door of hell. *See* W. E. H. Lecky: *History of European Morals* (Library edition), Vol. II, p. 357.

CHAPTER IV

CASTE

THE institution of caste occupies a most important place in the social organisation of India. It has come to be bound up with the Hindu religion and has pervaded many of the social conceptions of the Hindus and the codes of the Hindu law-givers. It has largely coloured their outlook on life. European and Indian scholars alike have described it as a unique institution peculiar to the soil of India. It is a vast and complicated subject which has given rise to a mass of speculation, ancient and modern. It excited the curiosity of the ancient sages and law-givers, travellers from foreign countries in the middle ages, European observers in modern times, the authors of our periodical census reports and European and Indian scholars interested in historical and sociological investigations. Let us, however, try and form a clear idea of caste. We are living in the midst of a caste organization which is all around us. We feel it and we have a conception of it. There is, however, considerable difficulty in formulating a scientifically precise definition of caste which will apply to all the groups which now consider themselves as separate groups with caste characteristics. We are concerned not so much with the sentiments or convictions or practices of individual members of the caste, but with the body of beliefs, sentiments and practices entertained or observed by the generality of the people belonging to the caste. The fissiparous tendency of the institution has manifested itself in the formation of a large number of sub-divisions, sects or groups bearing resemblance to each other in many respects, but separated by differences of language, residential areas and occupations. From a scientific point of view it might be useful to reserve the term 'caste' to indicate the main fundamental divisions and use other terms to denote the sects and sub-divisions. But no scientific terminology has been adopted in the vernaculars and by the people at large and the word commonly used by the people at the present time to indicate even the minor sub-divisions or groups is the word 'Jāti'. As applied to some of the smallest sub-divisions and groups, the ideas connoted by the common term 'Jāti' do not necessarily hold good in their entirety or with rigour. For instance, among the sub-division of the Tamil Brahmins known as Vaḍamas there is a distinction between the northern and the southern Vaḍamas. They were not generally in the habit, till recently, of inter-marrying with each other.

Prof. Rapson has adopted the definition of caste given in the Indian census report of 1911 as "an endogamous group or collection of such groups bearing a common name and having the same traditional occupation, who are so linked together by these and other ties, such as the tradition of a common origin and the possession of the same tutelary deity, and the same social status, ceremonial observances and family priests, that they regard themselves, and are regarded by others, as forming a single homogeneous community."[1] This definition is obviously loose and faulty. A common tutelary deity or a common set of family priests is not necessary for a common caste. The essential incidents of caste are the restrictions imposed by it upon inter-marriage, inter-dining and occupations. Numerous problems have been raised in connection with this subject and we shall refer to some of them to indicate the complexity of the subject. It is often said that caste is of Brahminical origin. Is this correct, and if so, in what sense and to what extent? Was caste based in its origin upon racial differences? Was there any caste among the Aryan invaders of India before they came to India, or did it come into existence for the first time after the invasion and settlement of the Aryans in India amongst the peoples of a different race or races? Was the institution the result of the development of certain universal instincts of human nature under specially favourable conditions in the new environment in which the Aryan invaders found themselves, or was it entirely the result of certain poisonous germs indigenous to the social atmosphere of India? Was caste the invention of a cunning priesthood deliberately planned to secure their own selfish purposes and imposed upon the rest of the population? If caste had its origin in a difference of colour or Varṇa, were the Dvijas or twice-born classes of the same colour or racial stock? If they were all

[1] *Cambridge History of India,* Vol. I, p. 53.

members of the same Āryan stock, when were the Brahmins, Kṣattriyas and Vaiśyas divided into the three separate Varṇas? Who were the Śūdras and was there any caste besides the Dvijas and the Śūdras? Were there any people who were not members of any caste at all, or who were literally outcastes, or did the outcastes themselves form a class? Were the social barriers and restrictions between the different castes rigid or flexible? If they were originally flexible, when did they become rigid? Has there been any large inter-mixture between the different castes and how far has it been recognised by law and custom? It is not possible to furnish any precise answer to all the questions I have indicated above and I do not propose to embark upon so extensive an inquiry.

We have already observed that the origin of caste engaged the speculations even of the ancient sages. The explanations given by them are mostly of a mythical or mystical character and sometimes rationalistic. The popular belief among Hindus is that the main divisions of castes are of immemorial antiquity and in fact coeval with creation. It is supported by the account in the Puruṣa Sūkta of the origin of the four castes from the mouth, arms, thighs and feet of Puruṣa, the Supreme Being. Obviously it is an allegorical account of the functions or occupations of the four castes and is clearly mythical. As pointed out by Sir W. Muir, no uniform or consistent account of the origin of the castes can be gathered from the

Hindu sacred books.[1] According to some accounts the four castes were derived from four different progenitors; according to others they were all descendants of Manu, the common ancestor of humanity. According to some, the castes were naturally distinguished by different Guṇas involving varieties of moral character; and according to others, mankind was originally endowed with the same uniform moral qualities, there being no distinction of classes, and the existing distribution has arisen out of differences of character and occupation. While it is true that the inter-mixture of castes has given rise to new castes, it is not possible to accept the theory contained in *Manu* which seeks to account for the origin not merely of castes, but of the racial divisions of mankind, like Yavanas (or Greeks), Śakas (or Scythians), Pahlavas and the Chinese, by supposing that they were Kṣattriya tribes who had gradually sunk to the condition of Śūdras as the result of their omission of their sacred rites and of their not consulting the Brāhmaṇas.[2] It is obvious that no weight can be attached to ethnological statements based upon such wild and fanciful conjectures. While the theories of origin embodied in such speculations cannot furnish any basis for rational conclusions, the Smṛtis furnish indirect indications with regard to the history of caste at different epochs. Valuable use has been made of the data contained in the Vedas, the epics and the

[1] For a summary of the accounts of the ancient Hindu writers, see Sir W. Muir: *Sanskrit Texts* (3rd edition), Vol. I, p. 159.

[2] *Manu*, X, 43-44.

Smṛtis by modern scholars, European and Indian. I will briefly refer to the conclusions which seem to emerge from their researches. Whether the caste system had been developed during the age of the Ṛg Veda has been a subject of controversy and it has been said that the Puruṣa Sūkta was a later composition than the bulk of the Ṛg Veda and cannot therefore prove the state of things which existed when the bulk of that Veda was composed. The Puruṣa Sūkta is obviously a speculation on a system which was flourishing at the time and the origin of which must have been lost in antiquity. It is difficult to accept the opinion of Prof. Rapson that the institution of caste is essentially of Brahminical origin and that it is based on the religious unity of the family symbolised by offerings to deceased ancestors and the doctrine of Svakarma.[1] (This word is used by Rapson. But 'Svadharma' is the more appropriate and commonly used term.) The Brahminical theories were either allegorical representations or speculative explanations of a pre-existing institution and the institution was not the consequence of the theory. The religious unity of the family and offerings to deceased ancestors were not confined to the Hindus or to India. They were to be found among the Romans and other nations also and the doctrine of Svakarma (or Svadharma) as a religious doctrine was rather the offspring than the parent of the institution of caste. According to Prof. Keith, there is no actual proof in the Ṛg Veda

[1] *Cambridge History of India*, Vol. I, p. 53.

that the priesthood was not then a closed hereditary class. There are traces of the division of the Āryan tribe into the "holy power (Brahman), the kingly power (Kṣatra) and the commonalty (Viś), and though the caste system was only in process of development in the Ṛg Veda, it seems impossible to deny that much of the groundwork upon which the later elaborate structure was based was already in existence."[1] The kingship was normally hereditary and there is no trace that the king was developed from the priest. According to E. Senart,[2] there is a distinction between Varṇa and Jāti, the former corresponding to class and the latter to caste. But the two words are generally used by Sanskrit writers in one and the same sense. Etymologically Varṇa indicated colour which depended on race, but as the Dvijas were in all probability of the same racial stock and divided only by occupation, they could not have formed three separate Varṇas or colours. The original divisions of Varṇas could have been only two, the fair-skinned Āryans and the dark-skinned Śūdras or Dasyus. When divisions of occupation led to separate groups and racial and occupational differences combined to help the formation of separate new groups, there must have grown up a tendency to use the words 'Varṇa' and 'Jāti' in the same sense of exclusive groups or castes. The notion of exclusive groups permeated even the Āryan Dvijas and the occupational divisions among them were also designated as Varṇas.

[1] *Cambridge History of India*, Vol. I, pp. 93-94.
[2] E. Senart: *Caste in India*, p. 128.

According to Mr. C. V. Vaidya, the Indian Aryans had already developed caste before the beginning of the epic period which he places at 3000 B.C., and the germs of caste were probably brought by the Indo-Aryans from their original home or developed during the Vedic period. Mr. Vaidya relies upon the facts admitted by Sir H. Risley that "among the Iranians there were four divisions of society, *viz.*, priests, warriors, agriculturists and artisans, and that the priests or the Atharvans did not generally give their daughters in marriage to the men of the lower classes."[1] The tendency to restrict marriages to the same class can be discovered among other communities belonging to the Aryan race, as for instance, among the Romans.[2] When the Aryans invaded India and settled in the Punjab, they were divided into three classes composed of the priest, the warrior and the agriculturist. The Śūdras or Dāsas were entirely of a different race and colour and they had to labour in the fields and

[1] C. V. Vaidya: *Epic India*, p. 53.

[2] Prejudices based upon colour or race are deep-rooted in human nature and have created a strong aversion to inter-marriages in modern times. Inter-marriages between Whites and Negroes have been the subject of statutory prohibition in America. "The Anglo-Saxon aversion to the black race is thus expressed by an English writer: 'We hate slavery, but we hate the Negroes still more'." (E. Westermarck: *The Origin and Development of the Moral Ideas*, Vol. I, p. 714.)

The German penal code has been recently sought to be revised on Nazi lines by declaring the invalidity of marriages between Germans and non-Aryans like Jews, Negroes and other coloured people. The intermingling of German blood with foreign blood communities or races is forbidden. Any sexual relationship between Germans and non-Aryans will be regarded as treason and punishable in the case of both parties.

do other menial work. The upper three classes were of the same race and colour and had marriage relations with one another. During this period which was anterior to the time of the *Manusmṛti*, a son born of a Brahmin from a wife belonging to any of the first three castes was a Brahmin. There were only four castes and a fifth did not exist.[1] At first the Aryans did not allow marriage relations with the fourth caste, *i.e.*, the Śūdras. There were exceptions to this rule, especially among the Vaiśyas or agriculturists who were in constant contact with the Śūdra or labouring class. Śūdra wives were taken rarely by the Brahmins, often by the Kṣattriyas and more frequently by the Vaiśyas. The practice which previously obtained among the Indo-Aryans *inter se* was for the progeny to follow the caste of the father. There was a repugnance to the application of this rule to the offspring of Śūdra wives. The Brahmins assigned a separate caste to such progeny and strongly interdicted such marriages. The next step was for the Kṣattriyas following the example of the Brahmins to prevent the son born of a Śūdra wife taking equal rank with sons of Kṣattriya wives. No separate name was assigned to the son of a Vaiśya by a Śūdra woman, probably because such inter-mixture of race was more pronounced in this case. The next step was to place a further restriction

[1] त्रिषु वर्णेषु जातो हि ब्राह्मणाद्ब्राह्मणो भवेत् ।
स्मृताश्च वर्णाश्चत्वारः पञ्चमो नाधिगम्यते ॥

Mahābhārata, Anuśāsanaparva, 47, 17-18.

upon the marriage of a Brahmin with a Vaiśya woman owing to the fact that the Vaiśya blood had lost its purity by inter-mixture. The son of a Brahmin by a Vaiśya wife was treated as a Vaiśya.[1] The son of a Brahmin by women of the first two castes was a Brahmin. But when more than one caste intervened between the Brahmin and his wife, the progeny was regarded as belonging to the caste of the mother. In the time of Manu probably and certainly in the days of Yājñavalkya the restrictions on marriage had made further progress and a separate caste was assigned to the son of a Brahmin by a Kṣattriya wife also. Mr. Vaidya's theory is supported by the passages to be found in *Manu* and other Smṛtis regarding the status of sons born of Anuloma marriages with wives of different castes. Originally the property of a deceased Brahmin had to be divided into ten shares, four were to go to the share of a son by a Brahmin wife, three to the son by a Kṣattriya wife, two to the son by a Vaiśya wife and one to the son by a Śūdra wife.[2] Pratiloma marriages were condemned and the progeny was generally despised as half-caste. The further development of caste grew apace with the spread of the Aryans in the country and the larger opportunities for contact between the Aryans and the Śūdras and aborigines.

Starting originally in difference of occupations

[1] भार्याश्चतस्रो विप्रस्य द्वयोरात्मा प्रजायते ।
आनुपूर्व्याद्द्वयोर्हीनौ मातृजात्यौ प्रसूयतः ॥

Mahābhārata, Anuśāsanaparva, 48, 4.

[2] *Manu*, IX, 153.

the conception of caste was modified by contact with people of alien races and colour after the invasion of India by the Aryans. Its further development was determined by considerations of racial purity or admixture. These factors and community of creed seem to me sufficient to account for the four main divisions of caste. The numerous fantastic ramifications of caste were determined by other considerations, such as residence in the same place, community of language, growing differences in occupations and the like. The Brahmins could not possibly have created the institution of caste, though they indulged in speculations and theories about the origin of caste and, like the priestly class in other countries, endeavoured to exalt the status of the priest and the warrior. It is also probable that when some of the non-Āryan races invaded India and were sufficiently assimilated to the people of the country in language, manners and customs, the Brahmins helped to discover pedigrees establishing the genealogical connection of the ruling families with the ancient Āryan chiefs of India.

It is pointed out by Mr. Vaidya that in king Harṣa's days a Kṣattriya could marry a Vaiśya woman and a Brahmin could marry a Śūdra woman. Bāṇa, the famous Sanskrit author, had two Pāraśava brothers, *i.e.*, born of a Brahmin father by a Śūdra wife. But at the time of Alberuni's visit (about 1030 A.D.) the practice of a Brahmin marrying outside his own caste had fallen into disuse.

It has been suggested by some social reformers that caste had originally nothing to do with birth and was merely a distinction based upon qualities, character and occupation. They rely upon a passage in the *Gītā*[1] and certain passages occurring in the *Mahābhārata*.[2] The verse in the *Gītā* merely states that the division into four castes was made by the Creator Himself with reference to the functional occupations of society and the innate qualities and dispositions of men befitting them for one or other of the functions. This verse must be regarded as a speculative account of the origin of the four main castes and contains a considerable measure of truth. But there can be no doubt that whatever the reasons for the origin of the system, castes soon became hereditary and more or less rigid. Fictions might have been occasionally adopted for the purpose of absorbing new tribes into a caste, but the theory has throughout been that the caste of an individual is determined by birth, *i.e.*, parentage. The considerations which furnished the historical origin of caste or which often led to the multiplication of castes have never affected, during the course of ages, the popular belief in the hereditary character of the institution. A person may of course lose caste by misconduct. There are also instances in the old legends of persons being exalted to a higher caste by virtue of their austerities. It is also stated in some of the Smṛtis that by inter-marriages in successive generations

[1] *Bhagavadgītā*, IV, 13.

[2] *See* verses 21, 23, 25, 26, 31-35 of Adhyāya 180, *Vanaparva*.

an exaltation or degradation of caste may be brought about.[1] The passages in the *Mahābhārata* which are relied upon contain a discussion between Nahuṣa (transformed into a python) and Yudhiṣṭhira as to how caste was to be determined. The answer given by Yudhiṣṭhira might at first sight seem to support the view that it was to be determined by character and conduct, but reading the passages as a whole, the proper interpretation seems to be that a Śūdra possessing the qualities and virtues of a Brahmin should be treated as a Brahmin and *vice versa*. There is a well-known maxim in Sanskrit that a fact cannot be altered by a hundred texts. The fact of parentage in a certain caste could not possibly be altered. But the social esteem of the individual would depend upon his character. If Yudhiṣṭhira meant to suggest that caste was determined simply by character and not by birth, the view is opposed to the facts of history. The verses dealing with this point start with the assumption that the individuals whose social position was considered were Śūdras and Brahmins.[2] Another conclusion which might be fairly drawn from the later verses in the same chapter is that where on account of the admixture of castes and irregular connections between them the paternity of an individual was not ascertainable, it should be inferred from his character and conduct and that membership of the twice-born classes was dependent not merely upon birth, but

[1] *Manu*, X, 42.

[2] *See* verse 25.

also upon the performance of the sacraments prescribed for the twice-born. While we may deplore the evil effects of the institution, it is not possible to entertain the view that social classifications were determined merely by character.

There were no serious restrictions upon inter-dining among the twice-born classes. According to the Smṛti of Vyāsa,[1] Dvijas can take meals with each other, and all that is necessary is that the person whose food one takes must be a member of a known family. The Smṛtis allowed the taking of food by Dvijas with certain classes of Śūdras also.[2] According to Gautama, a Brahmin may eat the food given by twice-born men who are praised for the faithful performance of their duties. He may also take food from a herdsman, a husbandman, an acquaintance of the family, a barber and a servant. If the means of sustaining life cannot be otherwise procured, they may be accepted from a Śūdra. Food brought unsolicited, small fish, venison, and roasted grain, if offered spontaneously by a man of any caste, must not be refused.[3] According to Āpastamba, pure men of the first three castes could prepare the food of the householder which is used at the Vaiśvadeva offering; or Śūdras may prepare the food under the superintendence of a man of the Ārya (*i.e.*, any of the first three) caste. If the food has been prepared by a Śūdra cook without supervision, it should be placed on the

[1] *Vyāsa*, III, 52.
[2] C. V. Vaidya: *History of Medieval India* Vol. II, p. 186.
[3] *Gautama*, XVII, 1-6.

fire and sprinkled with water and it is then fit for the gods.[1] According to Manu, the members of the Śūdra caste from whom a Brahmin may take food are a man's own cultivator, his family friend, his cowherd, his slave, his barber and a poor man who has taken service under him.[2] In the Dharmavyādha episode of the *Mahābhārata*, a Brahmin was advised by a Brahmin lady to seek knowledge of Dharma from a butcher and he accepted water at the hands of the butcher.[3] Udayanācārya, the author of the *Nyāyākusumāñjali*, who lived about the tenth century, complained that in his time there had been a degeneracy of the Brahmins in the matter of sexual relations and procreation, in the restriction of their studies to one Śākhā only of the Veda and in regard to their occupation and livelihood, and he stated that Brahmins had begun to take food even from Śūdras.[4] The restrictions in the matter of inter-dining must have become more stringent in subsequent times.

According to Manu, the three means of livelihood open to a Brahmin were teaching, officiating at sacrifices for others and accepting gifts from pure men. These were forbidden to a Kṣattriya and a Vaiśya. The profession of arms was a legitimate one for a Kṣattriya; and trade, agriculture and cattle-breeding were the prescribed

[1] *Āpastamba*, II, ii, 3, 1, 4, 9.
[2] *Manu*, IV, 253.
[3] *Vanaparva*, 207, 18.
[4] *Nyāyakusumāñjali, Stabaka II, Kārikā*, 3. (Chowkhamba edition, p. 56.)

occupations of a Vaiśya.[1] But if a Brahmin was unable to procure subsistence by his own special occupations, he could adopt any of the occupations of a Kṣattriya or a Vaiśya. It is very curious that even in cases where a Brahmin is reduced to the necessity of adopting these occupations, he is prohibited from the pursuit of agriculture, the reason being that it causes injury to many beings and requires external aid like bulls, implements, etc.; the ploughshare injures the earth and the beings living in the earth.[2] There is a very long and most curious list of exceptions.[3] A Kṣattriya is also permitted in distress to adopt the occupations open to a Vaiśya and a Vaiśya may subsist by following the occupations of a Śūdra.[4] But neither a Kṣattriya nor a Vaiśya is allowed to adopt any of the occupations of a higher caste, the penalty for a breach being deprivation of property and banishment.[5] A Śūdra who is unable to find service under the twice-born classes may in distress maintain himself by handicraft and may follow those mechanical occupations by following which the twice-born are best served.[6] It will be seen from a perusal of these rules and restrictions that they could not possibly have been strictly followed at any time and that they must have been more honoured in the breach than in the obser-

[1] *Manu*, I, 88-90. See also *Āpastamba*, II, v, 10, 4-7.
[2] *Ibid.*, X, 81-84. See also *Gautama*, VII.
[3] *Ibid.*, X, 85-94. See also *Gautama*, VII.
[4] *Ibid.*, X, 95, 98. See also *Gautama*, VII.
[5] *Ibid.*, X, 96.
[6] *Ibid.*, X, 99-100.

vance. In case of necessity a Brahmin may study even under a non-Brahmin. Considerable laxity seems to have grown up with regard to the pursuit of the prescribed occupations owing to the influence of Buddhism and economic necessity. The picture furnished by the Jātaka Tales of social and economic conditions shows many instances of such laxity.[1]

Outcastes seem to have always existed in society and to have been regarded as untouchable. According to Āpastamba it was sinful to touch, speak to or look at a Caṇḍāla, and penances were prescribed for this.[2] Yājñavalkya provided for the punishment of a Caṇḍāla who touched a man of the higher castes.[3] The Chinese Traveller Hieun-Tsang noticed the segregation of the outcastes outside towns and villages. The same thing was also noticed by Fa-Hian who states that the Caṇḍālas "live away from other people and when they approach a city or a market, they beat a piece of wood in order to distinguish themselves. Then people know who they are and avoid coming into contact with them."[4]

To understand the attitude of the Smṛti-writers with regard to the treatment of Śūdras, it is necessary to bear in mind that the Śūdras were different in colour and race from the Āryan settlers and had been conquered by the Āryans and reduced to servitude. The term 'Dāsa' or 'Dasyu' which was

[1] See *Cambridge History of India,* Vol. I, pp. 209-210.
[2] *Āpastamba,* II, i, 2, 8-9.
[3] *Yājñavalkya,* II, 234, 237.
[4] *Travels of Fa-Hian* (399-414 *A.D.*), re-translated by H. A. Giles, p. 21.

applied to them originally meant a foe. They were therefore treated as slaves or as members of a servile class and their primary duty was to serve the twice-born classes. Just as the Negroes were considered by the European settlers in America as the descendants of Ham meant under the curse pronounced by Noah to be kept in slavery, the Aryan settlers in India also set up the theory that the Śūdras were created to serve the twice-born classes.[1] The Śūdras were forbidden to study the Vedas and could acquire a knowledge of Dharma from the Purāṇas and other sources. According to the *Aitareya Brāhmaṇa*, a Śūdra is the servant of another liable to be expelled at will and to be slain at pleasure.[2] The Śūdra was created to be the slave of the Brahmin, and even if he is emancipated by his master, he is not released from his servile status.[3] A twice-born man is directed by Manu not to give advice to a Śūdra on secular or religious matters. According to Gautama, to

[1] *Cf.* the treatment accorded to the Bushmen in Africa and Australia by the European colonists and to the negroes in the Southern States of America (E. Westermarck: *The Origin and Development of the Moral Ideals*, Vol. I, pp. 370-371 and 712-714).

See also *Encyclopaedia of the Social Sciences*, Vol. XI, p. 339, *Negro problem*. "Discrimination against negroes took various forms, residential segregation, separation of the races in public conveyances and places of amusement, exclusion of negroes from public institutions and educational discrimination. Disfranchisement and social discrimination had their counterpart in all branches of industry except agriculture and domestic and personal service".

[2] *Aitareya Brāhmaṇa*, VII, xxix, 4.

It is reported by Lumholtz that once or twice colonists offered to shoot blacks for him so that he might get their skulls (E. Westermarck: *The Origin and Development of the Moral Ideas*, Vol. I, p. 371).

[3] *Manu*, VIII, 413-414.

defray the expenses of a wedding, a man may take money by fraud or force from a Śūdra.[1] "If a sacrifice offered by a twice-born man and especially by a Brāhmaṇa cannot be completed for want of any requisite, the article required for completion may be taken forcibly from the house of any Vaiśya who owns a large number of cattle, but does not perform the Soma or minor sacrifices. The Brahmin is also allowed to take at his pleasure two or three articles required for a sacrifice from the house of a Śūdra, since a Śūdra has no business with sacrifices. If a Dvija possessing a hundred cows does not kindle the sacred fire, or one possessing a thousand cows does not perform the Soma sacrifice, a Dvija who performs the sacrifice may unhesitatingly take the two or three articles from their houses, even though they be Brāhmaṇas or Kṣattriyas; or he may take by force or fraud from a Brāhmaṇa who always accepts and never gives and who refuses to give them. Thus the fame of the taker will spread and his merit increase."[2] Likewise he who has famished for three days may on the fourth day take what he requires for a day's subsistence either from a man who neglects his sacred duties or from the threshing floor or from a house or wherever he finds it. But if the owner should ask him, he must confess his deed and its causes. But on such occasions a Kṣattriya must never take the property of a virtuous Brāhmaṇa. If he is starving, he may appropriate things

[1] *Gautama,* XVIII, 24.
[2] *Manu,* XI, 11-15.

from a Śūdra or from a twice-born who neglects his duties.[1] And finally it is stated that "he who takes what is permitted by the texts on such occasions and bestows it on the virtuous becomes a raft enabling the owner to tide over the effects of his sin and the taker over his distress."[2] These extraordinary rules are deduced from the sacerdotal theory that "whatever exists in the world is the property of the Brāhmaṇa; on account of the excellence of his origin, the Brāhmaṇa is entitled to it all."[3] It is of course obvious that the object of this and other verses of a like character is merely laudatory and intended to indicate the exalted status of the Brāhmaṇa in the social order. The principle of exaggeration is often resorted to in the sacred books for the purpose of emphasising the merit or demerit of a person or an action, a virtue or a vice. Texts of this sort are intended to convey praise or censure and are treated as Arthavāda statements which have no obligatory force. They could only be invoked in favour of the ideal Brahmin who conducts himself according to the letter and the spirit of the sacred ordinances, and such Brahmins must, from the very necessities of the case, have been exceptionally few. It is further obvious that such rules could not possibly have been practically enforced at any time. But it cannot be denied that the differences in social status led to inequalities in the treatment of the different classes.

[1] *Manu*, XI, 16-18. See also *Gautama*, XVIII, 28-32.
[2] *Ibid.*, XI, 19.
[3] *Ibid.*, I, 100.

CHAPTER V.

SLAVERY

SLAVERY prevailed in most countries in the world and even among communities claiming to be civilised. Abundant evidence of its existence is to be found in the most ancient Hindu literature. Whenever a country was conquered by foreigners, the conquering nation or tribe reduced the inhabitants, or at any rate those who were taken captives in battle, to slavery. Seven kinds of slaves are referred to by Manu: he who is made a captive fighting under the standard of a defeated king, he who has become a slave for his subsistence, he who is born of a slave in the house, he who has been bought for a price, he who is given by his owner as a slave, he who has been inherited from ancestors as a slave and he who has been enslaved by way of punishment because he cannot pay a debt or fine.[1] A slave had no property and whatever he acquired belonged to his master. A Brahmin could under no circumstances be reduced to slavery. Though in strict theory the slave had no rights, his lot was mitigated in practice and the later Dharma Śāstras recognise the duty of a master to treat his slaves kindly. According to Āpastamba, a man may stint himself, his wife or his children in their food, but never a slave who does his work.[2]

[1] *Manu,* VIII, 415.

[2] *Āpastamba,* II, iv, 9, 11.

Manu laid down that a man must not quarrel with his slaves, since they follow him as his shadow.[1] As a slave possessed no property, he was liable to be taxed in manual labour.

According to the *Arthaśāstra* of Kauṭilya which probably depicts the state of things in the Maurya period, a slave may acquire property by his own labour performed without prejudice to his master. He may also acquire by inheritance from his father and he may redeem himself and become an Ārya again.[2] This probably refers to an Ārya or twice-born man who has become a slave and not to one of the aboriginal classes. This is also inferable from the passage which recognises the possibility of an Ārya mortgaging himself as a slave on account of distress or necessity. A man who robbed a slave of his wealth was liable to punishment. A slave might purchase his freedom by any earning acquired irrespective of his master's service, and ransom from outside could not be refused.[3] A female slave on whom a child had been begotten by her master and her child were entitled to freedom. If such a female slave attended to the affairs of her master's family or house after his death, even her brother, mother and sister earned their freedom, if they were slaves of the same master.[4] A fresh sale or mortgage of a slave after he or she had been redeemed from the

[1] *Manu,* IV, 180, 185.

[2] *Arthaśāstra* (Mysore edition), p. 182.

[3] *Ibid.*, p. 183.

[4] *Ibid.*, p. 183.

purchaser or pledgee was an offence, if the slave did not consent. A slave-child below eight years of age who had no relations could not be employed against his will in degrading occupations, nor sold or pledged in a distant country. Nor could a pregnant slave be sold or pledged without making provision for the expenses of her confinement. On the death of the slave, his property passed to his own kinsmen and it was only in default of such kinsmen that it went to the master.[1] A virgin slave who had been pledged and ravished by the pledgee was entitled to a Śulka or bride-price and the ravisher lost the amount of the pledge and paid a fine to the government.[2]

In course of time the position of the slave underwent further improvement. During the Buddhist period slaves do not appear to have been kept as a rule in great numbers either in the house or, as in the West, at mining or plantation work. Their treatment differed of course according to the disposition and capacity of both master and slave. The Jātaka Tales contain scarcely any evidence of ill-treatment and on the other hand the slave was often petted and permitted to learn writing and handicrafts, besides his ordinary duties as valet and foot-man. But if he committed a fault, he was liable to be beaten, imprisoned, branded and fed on slaves' fare.[3] The treatment of slaves in oriental countries and in Greece and Rome was generally

[1] *Arthaśāstra* (Mysore edition), p. 183.
[2] *Ibid.*, p. 182.
[3] *Cambridge History of India*, Vol. I, p. 205.

free from the cruelty and inhumanity which attended the treatment of negro slaves by the Christian nations of Europe. The facts adduced by E. Westermarck in his chapter on slavery amply justify his conclusion that the system of slavery which prevailed in the British colonies and in the slave States of North America surpassed in cruelty the slavery of any pagan country, ancient or modern.[1]

Considerable confusion has arisen from the practice of describing all Śūdras as Dāsas or slaves. Where whole tribes were reduced to subjection, the probabilities are that while some of the aboriginal inhabitants became slaves pure and simple of individual owners, the rest would rather stand in the relationship of unattached labourers or serfs, as conjectured by Prof. Keith.[2] Even those who were not serfs attached to any land would probably be in the position of mere labourers whose primary occupation would be to do service for the members of the twice-born classes and especially for the Brahmins. If a Śūdra was unable to find employment under them, he could adopt the profession of a Vaiśya and become a herdsman or a trader. A Śūdra who was unable to find service with the twice-born and threatened with the loss of his family through hunger might maintain himself by handicrafts.[3]

[1] *See* E. Westermarck: *The Origin and Development of the Moral Ideas,* Vol. I, pp. 704-714.

[2] *Cambridge History of India,* Vol. I, p. 129; Macdonell and Keith: *Vedic Index,* Vol. II, p. 388.

[3] *Manu,* X, 99.

CHAPTER VI.

LAW AND JUSTICE

THE social order of the Hindus was founded not upon the comparatively modern democratic principle of equality, but upon the conception of a social hierarchy based upon caste and sanctioned by religion. Though the Hindus attached the greatest importance to the virtues of justice and impartiality,[1] their conceptions were deeply permeated by the notion of inequality among the castes and sexes. The only way in which the social fabric could be maintained was by making every individual know his place in the social order and keep to it. While the principle of equality was applicable within the limits of each class or caste, the principle of discrimination was adopted as between one caste and another. While the relative estimation in which the three upper classes were held depended mainly upon the character of the occupations prescribed for or practised by them, the gulf which separated them from the Śūdras was due to racial considerations and the tendency to despise conquered peoples. The prestige and ascendancy of the higher classes could only be maintained by a differential treatment of the different castes. The notions of inequality between the different orders in social status were reflected in the administration of law and justice.

[1] *Manu*, VIII, 173.

Strange as it may seem to us who have been brought up in the modern notions of human equality and in the principles of the present-day English law which make no distinction between man and man, it does not require any imagination or research to realise the strength of the influence exercised by racial and aristocratic considerations, or the deeply rooted feeling of inequality between the sexes. It would be easy to collect numerous examples of discrimination in the administration of the law from systems ancient and modern, primitive and civilised.[1] Even in the time of the later Saṁhitās and Sūtras a differentiation was made in the wergeld payable for murder. The Sūtras fix the wergeld of a Kṣattriya at a thousand cows, of a Vaiśya at a hundred and of a Śūdra at ten, with a bull over and above for the king as a reward for his intervention.[2]

[1] In British India the Criminal Procedure Code in force till 1923 recognised racial distinctions, and European British subjects and other Europeans and Americans enjoyed special privileges. Even after the amendments introduced in the existing Criminal Procedure Code, this position of privilege is still maintained, though in an attenuated form. The recent deposition of Tshekedi, a ruling chief in Bechuanaland, for inflicting the punishment of flogging on a worthless European resident in native territory is an illustration of the length to which the representatives of the British Government are prepared to go in the maintenance of their racial prestige.

[2] *Apastamba*, I, ix, 24, 1-4; *Gautama*, XXII, 14-16.

Cf. "The laws of the Brets and Scots estimated the life of the King of Scots at a thousand cows; that of an earl's son, or a thane, at a hundred cows; that of a villein at sixteen cows. A similar system prevailed among the Celtic peoples generally, as also among the Teutons. A man's wergeld or life-price varied according to his rank, birth or office; and so minutely was it graduated, that a great part of many Teutonic laws was taken up by provisions fixing its amount in different cases. In English laws of the Norman age the *wer* or *villanus* is still only reckoned at £4, whilst that of the

The wergeld payable for women was the same as that fixed for a Śūdra.[1]

Distinctions were made both in civil and in criminal law between castes and sexes. The general principle adopted was that rights, duties and liabilities varied with caste or sex and punishments and damages were determined by the status of the accused or defendant and that of the complainant or plaintiff. The principle of discrimination was applied even with regard to the composition of the court, the competency of witnesses and the ordeals to be applied where evidence might be wanting. Though the system of caste had not attained full development or rigidity during the Vedic period, the social distinctions were well marked, especially those founded upon the difference of colour and race, between the invading Āryans and the original inhabitants whom they reduced to subjection. The remark of Prof. Keith that in the age of the later Saṁhitās the Brāhmaṇa had preference in his law cases is based upon his interpretation of a

homo plene nobilis is £25." (E. Westermarck: *The Origin and Development of the Moral Ideas,* Vol. I, p. 431.)

"From the beginning of the Empire (of Rome) the citizens were divided into privileged classes and commonalty—*uterque ordo* and *plebs*—and, whilst a commoner who was guilty of murder was punished with death, a murderer belonging to the privileged classes was generally punished with *deportatio* only. In the Middle Ages a similar privilege was granted by Italian and Spanish laws to manslayers of noble birth". (E. Westermarck: *The Origin and Development of the Moral Ideas,* Vol. I, p. 433.)

[1] *Bodhāyana,* I, x, 19, 3.

"According to Cambrian law the blood-price of a woman was half that of her brother." (E. Westermarck: *The Origin and Development of the Moral Ideas,* Vol. I, p. 420.)

passage in the *Taittirīya Saṁhitā*.[1] The real meaning of the passage seems to be the one adopted by Sāyaṇa in his Bhāṣya. Instead of referring to any litigation the passage seems to refer to a dispute between a Brahmin and a non-Brahmin regarding their relative superiority and the passage merely requires the referee of the dispute to support the claim of the Brahmin to superiority.

There were legal limits to the rate of interest to be taken from debtors and it varied according to the caste of the debtor from two per cent. per mensem in the case of the Brahmin debtor to three, four and five per cent. in the case of the Kṣattriya, Vaiśya and Śūdra.[2]

It is strange to find that, besides the remedy open to him in a court of justice, the creditor could also adopt various methods of self-help. He could have recourse to persuasion, to tricks, to force and to the customary practice of sitting in Dharṇa at the debtor's door and threatening to fast unto death. The debt due to a Brahmin had precedence even over the debt due to the king. But after the debts due to the Brahmin and to the king were discharged, the debts due to other creditors obtained priority in the order of time.[3]

[1] *Taittirīya Saṁhitā*, II, v. 11. *See* p. 203 of Prof. Keith's translation, Vol. 18, Harvard Oriental Series.

[2] *Manu*, VIII, 142; *Yājñavalkya*, II, 37.

[3] *Yājñavalkya*, II, 41.

To a charge of defamation, truth was no answer.[1] A Kṣattriya who defamed a Brahmin was liable to a fine of a hundred Paṇas, a Vaiśya to a fine of a hundred and fifty or two hundred Paṇas, and a Śūdra was liable to corporal punishment. But a Brahmin who defamed a Kṣattriya, Vaiśya or Śūdra was liable to a fine of fifty, twenty-five or twelve Paṇas. For defamation of a twice-born man by a man of an equal caste, the penalty was twelve Paṇas. A Śūdra who insulted a twice-born man with gross invective was liable to have his tongue cut off. If he mentioned the names and castes of the twice-born with contumely, an iron nail ten inches long should be thrust red-hot into his mouth, and if he arrogantly taught Brāhmaṇas their duty, the king should cause hot oil to be poured into his mouth and into his ears.[2] In case of assault, with whatever limb a man of the lowest caste caused hurt to a man of the three higher castes, that limb should be cut off. If he raised his hand or stick, he should have his hand cut off. If in anger he kicked with his foot, he should have his foot cut off. A low-caste man who tried to place himself in the same seat with a man of high caste should be branded on his hip and banished, or the king should cause his posteriors to be gashed.[3] One who kidnapped persons of

[1] See *Nārada*, XV-XVI, 21.

[2] *Manu*, VIII, 267-272.

[3] *Ibid.*, VIII, 279-281.

Cf. the provision of the Code of Louisiana that "free people of colour ought never to insult or strike white people nor presume to conceive themselves equal to the whites; but on the contrary,

noble family and especially women, or stole precious gems was liable to capital punishment.[1] According to Bṛhaspati, the kidnapper was to be burnt by the king with fire kept up with chaff.[2] For stealing goods belonging to Brāhmaṇas, for piercing the nostrils of a barren cow and for stealing other cattle belonging to Brāhmaṇas, the offender should lose half his foot.[3] With whatever limb a thief in any way committed an offence against men, he should be deprived by the king of that limb in order to prevent a repetition of the crime.[4] The king was required to leave no offender unpunished, whether the offender were a father, mother, wife, son, a teacher, a domestic priest or a friend.[5]

In the midst of all these differential rules of punishment, it is interesting to find a recognition in certain cases at least of the principle that the gravity of the offence increases in proportion to the status of the offender, as he is presumed to know the nature of the offence. In a case of theft, a Vaiśya and a Kṣattriya are liable to pay double and four times the fine payable by a Śūdra; but a Brāhmaṇa thief is liable to eight

they ought to yield to them on every occasion, and never speak or answer them but with respect, under the penalty of imprisonment, according to the nature of the offence." (E. Westermarck: *The Origin and Development of the Moral Ideas,* Vol. I, p. 714.)

1 *Manu,* VIII, 323.

2 *Bṛhaspati,* XXII, 18.

3 *Manu,* VIII, 325.

4 *Ibid.,* VIII, 334.

5 *Ibid.,* VIII, 335; *Mahābhārata, Sāntiparva,* 121, 60.

or even sixteen times the fine.[1] Where the king was himself an offender, he had to pay a thousand times the fine payable by an ordinary person.[2] In such a case the fine paid by the king should be either thrown into the water or distributed as gifts to Brāhmaṇas, the reason being that Varuṇa is the lord of punishment and punishes even kings, and that a Brāhmaṇa who has learnt the entire Veda is the lord of the whole world.[3]

A Brahmin was exempt from capital punishment,[4] but he was liable to be deported with his property.[5] In the exercise of self-defence a man may slay an assassin who approaches with a murderous intent, whether he be one's own teacher, a child, an aged man or a Brahmin deeply versed in the Vedas.[6] Adultery was generally punished with great severity. The king was recommended to adopt punishments which would strike terror.[7] Prisons were to be placed near a high road where the suffering and disfigured offenders could be seen by the passers-by.[8] The punishment for adultery except in the

[1] *Manu,* VIII, 337-338.

[2] *Ibid.,* VIII, 336.

[3] *Ibid.,* IX, 244-245.

[4] The immunities enjoyed by the Brahmins have some analogy to the benefits of clergy and other privileges enjoyed by the clergy and nobles in Europe. They were abolished in France by the revolution in 1789. The whole structure of medieval society in Europe was moulded in the spirit of caste. (*See* L. T. Hobhouse: *Morals in Evolution,* Vol. I, pp. 322, 324, 329.)

[5] *Manu,* VIII, 123-124, 380; see also *Arthaśāstra* (Mysore edition), p. 220.

[6] *Manu,* VIII, 350.

[7] *Ibid.,* VIII, 352.

[8] *Ibid.,* IX, 288. With the same object, the execution of certain

case of a Brahmin was death, for Manu says that the wives of all the castes must be carefully guarded.[1] A man of low caste who made love to a maiden of a higher caste was liable to corporal punishment.[2] The methods of punishment enjoined by the Smṛtis were barbarous and especially so in the case of sexual offences.[3] A woman guilty of adultery should be sentenced by the king to be devoured by dogs in a place frequented by many. The male offender was to be burnt to death.[4] A Śūdra who had intercourse with a woman of the twice-born classes was liable to be punished, if she was left unguarded, with the deprivation of the offending organ and all his property; and if she was guarded, with loss of everything, even his life.[5] Certain offences were regarded as mortal

prisoners condemned to death in Sind was carried out in public by the British authorities.

[1] *Manu*, VIII, 359.

[2] *Ibid.*, VIII, 366.

[3] *Cf.* "Mutilation or amputation of the offending member was a common form of punishment among the Greeks, Romans and Teutons. Medieval codes contain numerous instances of it." (E. Westermarck: *The Origin and Development of the Moral Ideas*, Vol. I, p. 521.)

The tortures applied to witches and to persons guilty of heresy were of fiendish cruelty. For an account of these tortures and of those employed in the administration of justice in the 16th, 17th and 18th centuries in Europe, see Preserved Smith: *A History of Modern Culture*, Vol. I, pp. 438, 439, 442, 463 and 496.

The brutal punishment of hanging, drawing and quartering was in force in England for the offence of treason till 1867. The last instance in which the sentence was carried out occurred in 1803. For the barbarity of the criminal law in Europe down to the nineteenth century refer to L. T. Hobhouse: *Morals in Evolution*, Vol. I, p. 112. *See also* E. Westermarck: *The Origin and Development of the Moral Ideas*, Vol. I, pp. 137-138.

[4] *Manu*, VIII, 371-372.

[5] *Ibid.*, VIII, 374.

sins causing a degradation of caste. The slayer of a Brāhmaṇa, a twice-born man who drinks spirituous liquor, he who steals the gold of a Brāhmaṇa and he who violates a Guru's bed are guilty of Mahāpātakas.[1] One of the punishments prescribed for these mortal sins is branding on the forehead with appropriate marks.[2] But the performance of the prescribed penances saved the offender from being branded, though not from liability to other punishments.[3] According to Nārada, if a member of a degraded class or an outcaste should insult a superior, he could be whipped on the spot by the man who was insulted. The king was also at liberty to whip him.[4] House-breakers by night should have their hands cut off and then impaled.[5] According to Bṛhaspati, house-breakers were liable to impalement and highwaymen to be hanged by the neck from a tree.[6] A cow-stealer should have his nose cut off and should be fettered and plunged into water.

It is interesting to note that the writers on Dharma Śāstra recognised a positive duty to render help on hearing a cry of distress from persons who were threatened with theft or violence from wild animals, or from flood or fire. A person who was able to render help but failed to do so was liable to punishment. Those who did not give assistance

[1] *Manu*, IX, 235.
[2] *Ibid.*, IX, 237.
[3] *Ibid.*, IX, 240.
[4] *Nārada*, XV-XVI, 11-14.
[5] *Manu*, IX, 276.
[6] *Bṛhaspati*, XXII, 17.

according to their ability when a village was being plundered, a dyke was being destroyed, or a highway robbery committed, should be banished with their goods and chattels.[1] According to Yājña-valkya, they were liable to a fine.[2] The *Arthaśāstra* of Kauṭilya contains more elaborate provisions on the subject. One who, being near, did not run to help another in danger was liable to punishment. Villagers on the banks of rivers were bound to rescue persons carried down by floods.[3] He who failed to run and help a man in the clutches of a tiger or other wild animal was also liable to punishment.[4]

We may refer to a few of the curious provisions in the criminal law laid down by the Smṛtis. A dishonest goldsmith should be cut to pieces with razors.[5] He who wantonly consorted with a widow, who being a Caṇḍāla touched men of the higher castes, who fed a Śūdra ascetic or Saṁnyāsin on religious or obsequial occasions, who, although disqualified, performed religious rites, was liable to a fine of a hundred Paṇas.[6] The penal laws contained in the *Arthaśāstra* of Kauṭilya are of considerable interest, as it is likely that they corresponded more closely to the actual administration of justice than the Smṛtis. Abuse of one's own country, village, caste or

[1] *Manu*, IX, 274.
[2] *Yājñavalkya*, II, 234.
[3] *Arthaśāstra* (Mysore edition), p. 206.
[4] *Ibid.*, p. 207.
[5] *Manu*, IX, 292.
[6] *Yājñavalkya*, II, 234-235.

society, temples and gods was an offence.[1] If a travelling merchant halted in a village and made his goods known to the headman and then suffered a loss of goods by theft or otherwise, the headman had to make good the loss. In certain other cases the owners or people of the village or the detective officer had to make good the loss.[2] Those who partook of prohibited food or drink were liable to be deported.[3] Various kinds of punishment were recognised by Kauṭilya, death by torture, impalement, burning of head and hands, drowning (for Brahmins), tearing by wild asses, or trampling to death by bulls, cutting off the tongue and mutilation. Kauṭilya winds up this chapter by saying that though these punishments of death by torture have been laid down by great sages, simple death is just in the case of offenders who have not been guilty of cruelty. According to him, accused persons were liable to torture of different kinds, if their answers to questions were unsatisfactory,[4] the object probably being to extract confessions.

Public servants who were guilty of misconduct in the discharge of their duties were, according to Kauṭilya, liable to punishment. The various kinds of misconduct on the part of a judge which rendered him liable to punishment were detailed at considerable length. "When a judge threatens, browbeats, sends out or

[1] *Arthaśāstra* (Mysore edition), p. 194.
[2] *Ibid.*, p. 232.
[3] *Ibid.*, p. 232.
[4] *Ibid.*, p. 218.

unjustly silences any one of the disputants in his court, he shall first of all be punished with the first amercement. If he defames or abuses any one of them, the punishment shall be doubled. If he does not ask what ought to be asked, or asks what ought not to be asked, or leaves out what he himself has asked, or teaches, reminds or provides any one with previous statements, he shall be punished with the middlemost amercement. When a judge does not inquire into necessary circumstances, inquires into unnecessary circumstances, makes unnecessary delay in discharging his duty, postpones work from spite, causes parties to leave the court by tiring them out by delay, evades or causes to evade statements that lead to the settlement of a case, helps witnesses giving them clues, or resumes cases already settled or disposed of, he shall be punished with the highest amercement. If he repeats the offence, he shall both be punished with double the above fine and dismissed."[1]

The rules laid down by Manu regarding the qualifications of witnesses are interesting. It is curious to note that among the competent witnesses special mention is made of men with male issue.[2] Among the persons who could not be summoned as witnesses are the king, a Śrotriya, a Vedic student, and an ascetic who has renounced the world, as these cannot be spared from their duties or occupations.[3] But there is a general rule that in all cases of

[1] *Arthaśāstra* (Mysore edition), p. 222.

[2] *Manu*, VIII, 62.

[3] *Ibid.*, VIII, 65.

violence, of theft and adultery, of defamation and assault, the rules about competency of witnesses must not be strictly applied. In case of a conflict of testimony, the king has to accept as true the evidence of the majority. It is only if the witnesses are equal in number, that the weight to be attached to the evidence depends upon the character of the witnesses.[1] The exhortation to the witnesses to speak the truth is most solemn and appeals to the strongest religious motives.[2] It is also interesting to note that after this collective appeal to the witnesses, the Brahmin witness is merely ordered to speak. It is presumed that this request is sufficient for a Brahmin to speak the truth. A Kṣattriya witness is ordered to speak the truth. A Vaiśya witness must be ordered to speak the truth

[1] *Manu,* VIII, 73.

[2] सत्यं साक्ष्ये ब्रुवन् साक्षी लोकानाप्नोति पुष्कलान् ।
इह चानुत्तमां कीर्तिं वागेषा ब्रह्मपूजिता ॥
साक्ष्येऽनृतं वदन् पाशैर्बध्यते वारुणैर्भृशम् ।
विवशः शतमाजातीस्तस्मात्साक्ष्यं वदेदृतम् ॥
सत्येन पूयते साक्षी धर्मः सत्येन वर्धते ।
तस्मात्सत्यं हि वक्तव्यं सर्ववर्णेषु साक्षिभिः ॥
आत्मैव ह्यात्मनः साक्षी गतिरात्मा तथात्मनः ।
मावमंस्थाः स्वमात्मानं नृणां साक्षिणमुत्तमम् ॥
मन्यन्ते वै पापकृतो न कश्चित्पश्यतीति नः ।
तांस्तु देवाः प्रपश्यन्ति स्वस्यैवान्तरपूरुषः ॥
द्यौर्भूमिरापो हृदयं चन्द्रार्काग्नियमानिलाः ।
रात्रिः सन्ध्ये च धर्मश्च वृत्तज्ञाः सर्वदेहिनाम् ॥

Manu, VIII, 81-86.

on pain of being visited with the sin of theft of kine, grain and gold; and a Śūdra witness should be ordered to speak the truth on pain of incurring the sin of all degrading crimes.[1] Brāhmaṇas who tend cattle, who trade, who are mechanics, actors (or singers), menial servants or usurers are to be treated by the judge like Śūdras.[2]

After this solemn exhortation, it is somewhat disconcerting to find that perjury from a pious motive is extenuated in certain cases.[3] Whenever the death of a Vaiśya, a Śūdra, a Kṣattriya or a Brāhmaṇa would be caused by declaration of the truth, a falsehood may be spoken, for such falsehood is preferable to truth. Such witnesses may expiate the guilt of the falsehood by certain penances.[4]

The Brahmin occupies a position of privilege in several respects. When a learned Brahmin finds a treasure trove, he may take the whole of it, for he is master of everything. When the king

[1] *Manu*, VIII, 88-101.

[2] *Ibid.*, VIII, 102.

[3] According to the early Christian church, all lies are not equally sinful. The degree of sinfulness depends on the mind of the liar and the nature of the subject on which the lie is told. Thomas Aquinas says that lying is not a mortal sin, if the end intended be not contrary to charity. The Greek fathers maintained that an untruth is not a lie when there is a 'just cause' for it; and as a just cause they regarded not only self-defence, but also zeal for God's honour. (*See* E. Westermarck: *The Origin and Development of the Moral Ideas*, Vol. II, pp. 99-101.)

"Jeremy Taylor asks 'who will not tell a harmless lie, to save the life of his friend, of his child, of himself, of a good and brave man?'" (E. Westermarck: *The Origin and Development of the Moral Ideas*, Vol. II, p. 104.)

[4] *Manu*, VIII, 103 ff.

finds a treasure trove, he must distribute half to Brahmins and put the other half into his treasury.[1] A Brahmin was also exempt from the payment of taxes and tolls.[2] On the death of a Brāhmaṇa without heirs, his property does not escheat to the king, but it must be distributed to learned and virtuous Brahmins, and if no such Brahmins are to be found, it should be distributed even to men who are members of the Brahmin caste.[3] Only a Brāhmaṇa could be appointed by the king to interpret the law and the king should under no circumstances allow a Śūdra to settle the law.[4]

[1] *Manu*, VIII, 37-38.
[2] *Ibid.*, VII, 133-136.
[3] *Ibid.*, IX, 189.
[4] *Ibid.*, VIII, 20.

CHAPTER VII

RIGHTS AND DUTIES OF RULERS AND SUBJECTS

According to the theory propounded in the *Manu-smṛti* and other Dharma Śāstras, the institution of kingship was created by God for the protection of the people and the king was allegorically represented as an incarnation of the eight guardian deities of the world.[1] He was therefore supposed to possess the powers of these divinities. The king was himself not above the law, but bound to observe and enforce the precepts of the Dharma Śāstra, and his subjects were bound to obey all lawful orders and decrees issued by him. He was bound to enforce law and justice, to uphold the laws of the country and castes and families, to protect the weak, the poor, the aged and the infirm, to refrain from oppression of his subjects, to defend his kingdom against aggression and to advance the interests of his people in all possible ways. Taxes were not to be oppressive and he was expected to raise revenue as the bees gather honey from the flowers.[2] The king was to associate with himself wise and learned counsellors and in important matters he convened assemblies of the people to ascertain their wishes, as King Daśaratha did when he intended to install Rāma

[1] *Manu,* V, 96; VII, 3-4.
[2] *Ibid.,* VII, 129.

as Yuvarājā. The revenue of the state is intended to be used for the benefit of the subjects and not to be spent merely for the pleasures of the king.[1] A king who oppressed his subjects incurred the risk of losing his life and kingdom.[2] It is laid down in the *Mahābhārata* that a king who, having promised to protect his subjects, fails to do so, should be killed by his combined subjects like a mad dog.[3] The duties of the rulers and their subjects were therefore reciprocal, the duty of allegiance being correlated to the duty of protection. The king was held by the people to be responsible even for the seasons. A drought or a famine was often believed to be the result of the king's maladministration or sins. The superstition sometimes went the fanciful length of attributing even premature deaths to the misdeeds of the king.[4] We may, however, be certain that this superstitious notion could hardly have been carried to its logical consequences.

We may refer to some of the rules concerning the duties of kings. The king was required to exercise a strict vigilance over all public servants. A low view was taken of the integrity of public officials. The system of espionage was generally adopted and spies are

[1] *Mahābhārata, Udyogaparva,* 118, 13-14.

[2] *Manu,* VII, 111.

[3] *Mahābhārata, Anuśāsanaparva,* 61, 33.

[4] The belief that national catastrophes are inflictions for the vices or the religious errors of leading men has been entertained in European countries also. *See* W. E. H. Lecky: *History of European Morals* (Library edition), Vol. II, p. 236.

generally described as the eyes of the king. The king was required to appoint a loyal minister to supervise the conduct of affairs by the administrative heads of groups of villages and in every town he had to appoint a high official to superintend all affairs. It is interesting to note the reason for this close supervision. Manu says that the servants of the king who are appointed to protect the people generally become corrupt knaves and the subjects should be protected against them. Those officials who took bribes from suitors were to be banished from the kingdom and their property was to be confiscated.[1] Those who were guilty of treason by serving the king's enemies, those who corrupted his ministers and those who forged royal edicts were to be put to death. The methods adopted for the detection of crimes included the employment of spies, of old reclaimed thieves and other disreputable characters and the instigation through the agency of the police and bad characters of suspected persons to commit crimes. The spies and other detective officers were to assume disguises, consort with the suspected persons and induce them to commit crimes. They were to be inveigled into the presence of the officers of justice, but if they scented danger and refused to come, they were to be attacked and slain, together with their friends, blood relations and connections.[2]

There is a chapter in Kauṭilya's *Arthaśāstra* which deals with the various methods of getting

[1] *Manu*, VII, 123-124.
[2] *Ibid.*, IX, 259-272.

rid of courtiers and officials suspected of treason and other seditious persons. The intrigues and plots which are recommended for this purpose are of a Machiavellian character.[1] The depravity of the standard of morality displayed in these maxims of the *Arthaśāstra* surpasses one's imagination and it is to be hoped that it was not characteristic of the methods ordinarily adopted by kings for dealing with persons of these classes, but referred rather to the disturbed condition of the age in which the *Arthaśāstra* was composed. As is usual in the case of all despotic monarchies, the king was living in an atmosphere of intrigue and in constant fear of treachery. The food of the king had to be previously examined and hallowed by sacred texts that destroy poison. His food was to be mixed with antidotes against poison and he was to be careful to wear gems which destroy poison. The dress and ornaments of his female attendants should be carefully searched to guard against the possibility of their concealing poison or weapons. He had to observe similar precautions with regard to his carriage, bed, seat, bath, toilet and all his ornaments.

It is interesting to notice that courtesans were often utilised by the criminal investigation department in the detection of offences. There was a public officer appointed in the time of the *Arthaśāstra* for the superintendence of prostitutes. There is a whole chapter in the *Arthaśāstra* containing elaborate provisions on this subject. Those who taught the fine arts and other accomplishments to

[1] See *Arthaśāstra* (Mysore edition), pp. 236-240.

prostitutes, female slaves and actresses were to be provided with maintenance from the state. Another extraordinary provision was that if a prostitute did not yield her person to anyone under the orders of the king, she was liable to a sentence of a thousand lashes with a whip or a fine of five thousand Paṇas.[1]

The vice of gambling was not unknown to the ancients even in the age of the Ṛg Veda. The evil was deplored and reprobated, and the lament of the gambler is the subject of a beautiful hymn in the Ṛg Veda.[2] Gambling and betting were considered most serious vices and the king was required by Manu to spare no pains in suppressing them. Gambling was known to have produced great enmity in a former age. It was regarded as equivalent to open theft.[3] The difference between gambling and betting (Dyūta and Samāhvaya) was that the term 'gambling' was used where inanimate things like dice, staves of ivory or bits or slices of leather were used, and the term 'betting' was used where birds or animals were the subject of wager. The king was required to suppress these two vices and those addicted to them were to be sentenced to corporal punishment and immediate banishment. Later law-givers preferred the policy of regulation to that of prohibition. Suppression of a generally prevalent instinct was found impracticable and it was considered the wiser course to adopt a system of licens-

[1] *Arthaśāstra* (Mysore edition), p. 125.

[2] *Ṛg Veda*, X, 34.

[3] *Manu*, IX, 222, 227.

ing and control and turn it to public uses by making it a source of revenue and a help to the detection of crime. According to Āpastamba, the king was to build an assembly house at some distance from the town with doors on all sides and erect a gaming table there. Men of the first three castes who were pure and truthful were allowed to play there.[1] According to the *Arthaśāstra,* the keeper of a gaming house should allow gambling only in one place under his supervision to enable him to help in the detection of those who live by underhand means. He has to supply proper dice at a fixed charge and is to take from the winner five per cent. of the stakes, the hire of the dice and other accessories and a charge for supplying water and accommodation and for the licence.[2] In another chapter there is an interesting discussion by Kauṭilya of the vices to which men are addicted and he considers the relative evils of gambling and drinking, and he seems to think that gambling is the worse of the two evils.[3] Yājñavalkya also provides for the regulation of gaming houses. The keeper of a gaming house should take from a gambler five per cent. when the stakes amount to a hundred or more and ten per cent. in other cases. The gaming house is protected by the king and the keeper must pay the appointed share of the profits to the king. The payment of the stakes can be enforced by the winner only when the game has been played in a public assembly of gamesters in the presence of the keeper

[1] *Āpastamba,* II, x, 25, 12-13.
[2] *Arthaśāstra* (Mysore edition), pp. 197-198.
[3] *Ibid.,* p. 328.

and of the king's superintendent and the king's share has been paid. Those who played with false dice should be branded and banished. Gaming was to be allowed only under the supervision of a single authority, so that it might be a means of detection of thieves.[1] The master of a gaming house should arrange the game and pay the stakes to the winners. He is himself entitled to a profit of ten per cent. Those who gamble must either get a licence from the king or pay to the king the share due to him and play in public. A man who has not paid his debts incurred in gambling is not permitted to enter another gaming house. They were regarded as debts of honour which a man must pay of his own accord.[2] Bṛhaspati refers to the prohibition of gambling and betting by Manu because it destroys truth, honesty and wealth. But it was permitted by other law-givers when conducted so as to allow the king a share of every stake.[3] One who was defeated in a secret game or was ignorant of the rules, or though acquainted with the game has lost by foul play, should be released and one who has forfeited his entire wealth in a game should not be compelled to give the whole of it.[4]

According to Bodhāyana, the drinking of spirituous liquor was a heinous offence on the part of a Brahmin and he was to be branded with the sign of a tavern and banished.[5] The religious penance

[1] *Yājñavalkya*, II, 199-203.
[2] *Nārada*, XVII, 2, 5, 7, 8.
[3] *Bṛhaspati*, XXVI, 1.
[4] *Ibid.*, XXVI, 7.
[5] *Bodhāyana*, I, x, 18, 18.

prescribed was to pour hot spirituous liquor into his mouth. Various penances are prescribed by Manu for a Brahmin who has intentionally drunk spirituous liquor, to expiate his sin. One of the methods of expiation prescribed is to drink red-hot boiling liquor till he is scalded to death.[1] According to the *Arthaśāstra,* elaborate provisions are to be made in the excise department for the regulation of the manufacture, consumption and sale of liquor. For consumption outside a shop, liquor was to be sold only to men who were well known and of good character. The liquor shops too were to be utilised for the detection of offenders and bad characters. Liquor could not be sold below its price and bad liquor could be given only to slaves or workmen in lieu of wages or to draught animals and hogs. The taverns should contain apartments with separate beds and seats. The drinking saloons were to be adorned with flowers, filled with scents, and made comfortable according to the season. The police should employ spies in the shops to watch the character and movements of the customers.[2]

Aggressive wars were not forbidden and territorial aggrandisement or extension of sovereignty was a legitimate ambition in a king. When he gained a victory, he must proclaim the safety of the inhabitants of the conquered territory. After ascertaining the wishes of the people in the conquered state, he must place a member of the family of the deceased ruler on the throne, imposing his own

[1] *Manu,* IX, 235, 237; XI, 91.

[2] *Arthaśāstra* (Mysore edition), p. 119.

conditions upon him. He must maintain the laws and customs of the conquered country and honour the new king and his ministers and important officials with precious gifts.[1]

We may now pass on to the principles of ethics governing the conduct of duels and battles and wars. A distinction must here be made between the principles applicable to single combats or duels and those applicable to the conduct of war. In laying down the duties of a king, Bodhāyana says that he should not turn back in battle and should not strike with barbed or poisoned weapons. He must not fight with those who are in fear, intoxicated, insane or out of their minds, nor with those who have lost their armour, nor with women, nor with infants, aged men or Brāhmaṇas who are not assassins.[2] Āpastamba declares that the Āryas forbid the slaughter of those who have laid down their arms, of those who beg for mercy with flying hair or joined hands and of fugitives.[3] The rules contained in the *Manusmṛti* are more elaborate. When a king fights with his foes in battle, he must not strike with concealed weapons (like a sword-stick), nor with such as are barbed or poisoned or the points of which are blazing with fire. He may not strike a dismounted enemy, nor a eunuch, nor one who supplicates with folded hands, nor one who flees with flying hair, nor one who has sat down, nor one who has surrendered himself as a captive,

[1] *Manu*, VII, 201-203.
[2] *Bodhāyana*, I, x, 18, 9-12.
[3] *Āpastamba*, II, v, 10, 11.

nor one who is sleeping, nor one who has lost his armour, nor one who is naked, nor one who is without weapons, nor one who looks on without taking part in the fight, nor one engaged with another antagonist, nor one whose weapons are broken, nor one afflicted with sorrow, nor one who has been grievously wounded, nor one who is in terror, nor one who has turned back from the field. In all these cases the king should remember the duty of honourable warriors.[1] These are the rules laid down for all Kṣattriyas engaged in battles. It must be remembered that according to the Indian methods of battle, warriors were often engaged in single combats and hand to hand fights and the principles above referred to were applicable to these cases. But in the conduct of a campaign recourse was often had and allowed to stratagems and rules of warfare which did not lean on the side of leniency. A king may besiege his enemy, devastate his country and spoil his supplies, grass, fuel, food and water. He may also destroy the enemy's tanks, ramparts and ditches, attack him unawares and alarm him at nights. He may also instigate the enemy's subjects to revolt. As victory in an engagement is always uncertain, he must avoid fighting as far as possible and must seek to attain his object by conciliation or gifts or by fomenting dissensions in the enemy's ranks. But if the other three methods fail, he must fight to conquer.[2] A righte-

[1] *Manu,* VII, 90-93.
[2] *Ibid.,* VII, 195-200.

ous battle was considered the highest good for a Kṣattriya.[1] Death in the battlefield should be welcome to the warrior and death in his own home should be regarded as inglorious. The ethics of honourable warfare laid down for the Kṣattriyas have seldom been equalled and never surpassed by any code of chivalry in the world. It must not, however, be supposed that this ideal was invariably or strictly observed. There were occasional lapses, as for instance in the case of Bhīma who killed his adversary Duryodhana by hitting him in the thigh. Duryodhana's mother, Gāndhārī, reproached Bhīma for hitting her son below the belt. Bhīma tried to defend himself on two grounds, on the ground that he was driven to do so as a matter of sheer necessity and self-protection against a foe of superior strength and also on the ground that, Duryodhana having insulted Draupadī by inviting her to sit on his lap and baring his thigh for the purpose, the punishment was appropriate to the offence.[2]

It is laid down in the *Mahābhārata* that a wounded enemy should either be restored to his own home or treated in the conqueror's country and discharged after recovery.[3]

[1] *Bhagavadgītā*, II, 31.

[2] *Mahābhārata, Strīparva*, 15, 2-10.

[3] चिकित्स्यः स्यात्स्वविषये प्राप्यो वा स्वगृहे भवेत् ।
निर्व्रणश्च स मोक्तव्य एष धर्मः सनातनः ॥

Mahābhārata, Śāntiparva, 95, 13-14.

CHAPTER VIII

MISCELLANEOUS TOPICS

Ahiṁsā

It has generally been recognised to the credit of the Hindu religion that kindness to animals has been inculcated as a sacred duty. It is unnecessary to seek an explanation for this precept in the doctrine of transmigration of souls. The sanctity attached to all kinds of life and the duty of abstaining from any form of injury or hurt to living beings and showing compassion to all animals down to the smallest creatures was one of the essential tenets of Hinduism.[1] It is a mistake to suppose that the doctrine of Ahiṁsā was for the first time taught by Buddha and that the Brahmins borrowed the doctrine from Buddhism. What was novel in Buddha's teaching was not the doctrine of Ahiṁsā or compassion to living beings, but his condemnation of blood sacrifices. The slaughter of animals as a sacrifice to the gods was part of the old Vedic religion as of most other primitive religions in the world and it was regarded as one of the few lawful exceptions to the injunction against the taking of life. The injunction was particularly stringent in the case of the Brahmin. To what fanciful lengths it was preached is

[1] For the attitude of Christianity towards lower animals *see* E. Westermarck: *The Origin and Development of the Moral Ideas,* Vol. II, pp. 506-514.

apparent from the prohibition of agriculture as a profession for the Brahmin on the ground that ploughing would involve injury to the numerous living creatures in the soil. Even the fowler who shot a bird while it was mating was cursed by Vālmīki for his sin.[1] Though the Lord Buddha laid stress upon the importance of compassion and Ahiṁsā, neither he nor his followers had any objection to the use of meat. Boar's flesh was eaten by Buddha himself[2] and it is even alleged that he died of a surfeit of pork. Three pure kinds of flesh were allowed to the Buddhist monks, *viz.*, unseen, unheard, or unsuspected. Buddha declared that they were not to eat the flesh of any animal which they had seen put to death for them or about which they had been told it had been killed for them or about which they had reason to suspect that it had been slain for them.[3] Flesh not coming within these three categories was lawful for them. Buddha sanctioned the use of flesh as an ordinary food by his own example and implied permission. But when some of his disciples gave offence by begging for beef and mutton and asking to have animals killed for them and eating as daily food flesh which is only to be taken under exceptional circumstances, he introduced a prohibition. In no Buddhist country in the world have the people generally abstained from the use of meat. On the other hand, the strictest vegetarians in the

[1] *Rāmāyaṇa, Bālakāṇḍa,* 2, 15.

[2] Sacred Books of the East Series, No. XI, *Buddhist Suttas,* pp. 71-73.

[3] Thomas Watters: *Yuan Chwang,* Vol. I, p. 55.

world are to be found among the Brahmins in the Madras and Bombay Presidencies, the Banias in western and upper India and the Jains.

Notwithstanding the inculcation of Ahiṁsā as one of the highest virtues, we find that from the earliest times animals have been used for food by Hindus of many classes, including even Brahmins, in former times. There is some difficulty in reconciling the slaughter of animals for food with the principle of Ahiṁsā. So far as sacrifices to the gods were concerned, they were justified on the authority of Vedic injunctions. The only explanation seems to be that the ancient Hindus did not regard the killing of animals for food as unlawful, provided it was done without needless cruelty. The slaying of a big ox or a big goat for guests was prescribed in the Vedas[1] and the injunction has been repeated in the Smṛtis also. The great Yājñavalkya was wont to eat the meat of milch cows and bullocks, if only it was Aṁsala (firm or strong). Oxen were also slaughtered for food at marriages. On account of the value of the cow for other purposes than flesh-eating, the cow was acquiring a special sanctity and was called Aghnyā (not to be slain). Gautama laid down that small fish and venison offered by a man of any caste must not be refused by a Brahmin. There was a general prohibition against the eating of five-toed animals with certain exceptions, which included the porcu-

[1] *Satapatha Brāhmaṇa*, III, iv, 1, 2.
Sāṅkhyāyana Gṛhya Sūtra, II, xv, 2.

pine, the hare, the tortoise, the iguana and the rhinoceros. Milch cows and draught oxen were prohibited as food[1] on account of their obvious utility, a clear indication that other kinds of cows and bulls might be taken. Āpastamba declared which kinds of flesh, fish and birds might be eaten and which not.[2] It is noteworthy that the meat of milch cows and oxen were permitted to be eaten. Bodhāyana also gives a list of the animals whose flesh may be eaten, which among others includes the spotted deer, the buffalo and the wild boar.[3] Vasiṣṭha allowed the use of the flesh of certain animals, but disapproved of the flesh of milch cows, draught oxen and animals whose milk teeth have not dropped.[4] The rules laid down by Manu are contradictory. The grounds on which he disapproves of the use of meat are set forth in Chapter V, Ślokas 45 to 55. "Meat can never be obtained without injury to living creatures, and injury to sentient beings is detrimental to the attainment of heavenly bliss. A twice-born man must therefore shun the use of meat. Having well considered the disgusting origin of flesh and the cruelty of fettering and slaying corporal beings, he must abstain from eating flesh. He who permits the slaughter of an animal, he who cuts it up, he who kills it, he who buys or sells meat, he who cooks it, he who serves it up and

[1] *Gautama,* XVII, 3, 27-31.
[2] *Āpastamba,* I, v, 17, 29-39.
[3] *Bodhāyana,* I, v, 12, 6.
[4] *Vasiṣṭha,* XIV, 39, 45.

he who eats it must all be considered slayers of the animal. There is no greater sinner than the man who, though not worshipping the gods or the manes, seeks to increase his own flesh by the flesh of other beings."[1]

Strangely enough, in the course of the same chapter there are several verses recognising the lawfulness of animal food without any attempt at reconciliation. As the use of meat is ordained in sacrifices and on occasions of Śrāddha to the manes, he declares that one who eats meat when he honours the gods and manes commits no sin, whether he has bought it or has himself killed the animal or has received it as a present from others. A twice-born man who, being duly engaged to officiate or dine at a sacred rite, refuses to eat meat becomes an animal after death during twenty-one existences.[2] The things which a twice-born man should not refuse, if voluntarily offered, include fish and meat.[3] One may eat meat over which water has been sprinkled with recitation of Mantras, when Brāhmaṇas desire one to do it, when one is engaged in the performance of a rite according to the sacred law or when one's life is in danger.[4] The Lord of Creatures, Prajāpati, created the whole world for the sustenance of life. Both the movable and the immovable creation is food for the living.[5] What is

[1] *Manu,* V, 48, 49, 51, 52.
[2] *Ibid.,* V, 31-36.
[3] *Ibid.,* IV, 250.
[4] *Ibid.,* V, 27.
[5] *Ibid.,* V, 28.

destitute of motion is the food of those endowed with locomotion; animals without fangs are the food of those with fangs; those without hands, of those who possess hands; and the timid, of the bold.[1] The eater who even daily devours those destined to be his food commits no sin, for the Creator himself created both the eaters and those who are to be eaten.[2] The gods declared three things to be pure to Brāhmaṇas, *viz.*, that on which no taint is visible, that which has been washed with water and that which has been commended as pure by the word of a Brāhmaṇa.[3] His final view seems to be that there is no sin in eating meat, in drinking wine or in carnal intercourse, for that is the way of all creatures, but abstention brings great rewards.[4]

In the episode of the virtuous butcher in the *Mahābhārata,* the butcher was selling pork and buffalo's flesh. He was himself not a flesh-eater and never killed animals. He merely sold the flesh of animals killed by others and was only following his hereditary profession. The virtues cultivated by him were truth-speaking, freedom from envy, liberality and hospitality. In Ślokas 23 to 29 of Chapter 208 of the *Vanaparva* there is an elaborate justification or apology for the slaughter of animals for food. It points out the impossibility of avoiding the sin of killing any kind of creature and comes to the conclusion that

[1] *Manu*, V, 29.
[2] *Ibid.*, V, 30.
[3] *Ibid.*, V, 127.
[4] *Ibid.*, V, 56.

where it is so difficult to lay down the principles of Dharma, he who performs his appointed duty is free from sin.

Aśoka made regulations restricting the slaughter of animals for food and especially on occasions of festivals and public shows.[a] We have references in his edicts to show that his appeal to the people and the ordinances he issued for the prohibition of killing of animals met with a ready response and that the people generally abstained from taking life. King Harṣa also prohibited all animal slaughter.[2] There are numerous other restrictions on diet in the Dharma Śāstras, some of which are reasonable and conformable to rules of hygiene, some admit of an explanation and others can only be regarded as superstitious taboos.

Cleanliness.

More than any other religion Hinduism laid stress upon the importance of cleanliness and purity of body as well as mind. It may even be said that the emphasis laid upon cleanliness is carried to the point of exaggeration. But it is better to exaggerate than underrate the virtue of cleanliness. It cannot be said that in laying stress upon the virtue of cleanliness of the body, the Hindu law-givers did not adequately appreciate the greater importance of purity of mind and character. Gautama declares that a man who is sanctified by the forty sacraments detailed by him,

[1] *Cambridge History of India*, Vol. I, p. 496.
[2] C. V. Vaidya: *History of Medieval India*, Vol. I, p. 105.

but who is devoid of the eight virtues of compassion towards all creatures, forbearance, freedom from anger, purity, quietism, auspiciousness,[1] freedom from avarice and freedom from covetousness, cannot reach heaven or obtain union with Brahman.[2] Manu states that he is pure who gains wealth with clean hands and not he who purifies himself with earth and water.[3]

Foreign languages and travel.

Restrictions were imposed upon learning the language of Mlecchas or barbarians.[4] Viṣṇu says that after speaking to a barbarian or a Caṇḍāla a man must clean his mouth by Ācamana or the sipping of water.[5]

Sea-voyages were forbidden by Bodhāyana.[6] He was of opinion that making voyages by sea caused a loss of caste. He mentions, however, that the practice of going to sea was one of the customs peculiar to the north of India.[7]

Penances.

Most systems of ecclesiastical law include the subject of penances for sins. Sins and crimes largely overlap each other. The same act or omission may constitute a sin from the religious point

[1] The word Maṅgalya in the original is interpreted to mean 'right conduct'.

[2] *Gautama,* VIII, 23-25.

[3] *Manu,* V, 106.

[4] *Vasiṣṭha,* VI, 41.

[5] *Viṣṇu,* XXII, 76.

[6] *Bodhāyana,* II, i, 2, 2.

[7] *Ibid.,* I, 1, 2, 4.

of view, a wrong from the point of view of morality, or an offence from the legal point of view. It is not surprising that in the system of the Dharma Śāstra which deals with duties of all kinds and their violations and which mixes up the subjects of law, religion and morality, we should find sanctions of all kinds, secular punishments by the arm of the king, penances in this life and punishments in a future life. Whether an offender would be cumulatively liable to all these forms of punishment, or whether the infliction of punishment by the king would absolve the offender from future punishment or the performance of a penance, or whether the performance of a penance would absolve the offender from liability to punishment by the king or from future punishment are interesting questions upon which it is not possible to give definite answers with confidence. The general principle that a man should not be punished twice for the same wrong is so conformable to our common sense that we cannot suppose it to have been absent from the minds of the Hindu Smṛti-writers. Evidence is not wanting of the recognition of this principle in the Dharma Śāstras. It is of course possible to suggest that the object of a penance prescribed by religious authority is to absolve the wrong-doer from sinfulness and reform his character and that the objects of secular punishment are to enforce retribution and to deter other persons from committing similar wrongs. The reformation of the character of the offender no doubt plays a part in the theory of criminal justice, but the other two objects in the theory of secular punishment cannot be equally satisfied by the mere performance of penances. It may be reasonably held that the performance of a penance should not save the wrong-doer from punishment by the king, especially when we remember that several of the penances prescribed are comparatively light and consist in the making of gifts to Brāhmaṇas. Having regard to the absence of any organised machinery for the enforcement of penances, to their variable character and to the uncertainties of their operation, they should not be allowed to be pleaded as a substitute for secular punishment. Similarly it may be contended that the suffering of the punishment inflicted by the courts cannot dispense with the necessity for the performance of a penance. From the point of view of punishment in a future life, as the object of a penance is to wash out the sin of the wrong-doer, he should not be made liable to future punishment after the performance of the prescribed penance in this world. In so far as the objects of secular punishment include the reformation of the offender's character, the suffering of punishment under the sentence of the king should also logically exonerate the offender from future punishment, unless his character remains unreformed. "Men who have committed crimes and have been punished by the king become pure and go to heaven, like those who perform meritorious deeds."[1] There are, of course, cases where an act or omission may not be punishable by

[1] *Manu*, VIII, 318.

the criminal law at all and the offender is only liable to a penance or to a future punishment. In all such cases it is only just and reasonable that the performance of the prescribed penances should be a complete absolution from all punishment in a future existence. Abuses have crept into every ecclesiastical system of penances and it cannot be claimed that the Hindu system has been free from such abuses any more than the Christian church. But it would be a mistake to imagine that according to the Dharma Śāstras a penance could be efficacious, if it was not accompanied by a change in the will, disposition and character of the wrongdoer. The theory of penances is laid down in *Manu*. Certain kinds of intentional and deliberate offences like the slaying of a Brahmin without good cause cannot be expiated by any penance. The view that only unintentional offences can be expiated is unwarranted and absurd. It may very well be argued that an unintentional act or omission cannot and ought not to be regarded as an offence at all. But just as for the purposes of the civil law a man may be liable for an unintended injury to another in certain cases, the writers on Dharma Śāstra have taken the view that even an unintentional wrong entails in certain cases liability to a penance. Wherever a penance is prescribed specifically or in general terms, the mere performance of it in the letter has no efficacy. "A sinner is freed from guilt by confession, repentance, austerities and recitation of the Veda, and in case of impossibility (if the offender is unable to perform the penances or to recite the Vedic texts), by gifts. In proportion as a man who has done wrong himself confesses it, even so far he is freed from guilt as a snake from its slough. In proportion as his heart loathes his evil deed, even so is his body freed from that guilt. He who has committed a sin and has repented is freed from that sin, but he is purified only by the resolution of ceasing to sin and thinking 'I will do so no more'. Having thus considered in his mind what results will arise from his deeds after death, let him always be good in thought, speech and action. He who, having either unintentionally or intentionally committed a reprehensible deed, desires to be freed from the guilt of it, must not commit it a second time. If his mind be uneasy with respect to any act, he must repeat the austerities prescribed as a penance for it, until his conscience is fully satisfied."[1] The doctrine of expiation by penances found a place in Christianity also. But the Hindu law-givers never went the same length as the Christian church which in the Council of Trent pronounced an anathema on those who asserted that true repentance was shown in a new life rather than in the performance of penances.

When from the theory of penances we go into the details of the penances prescribed for different persons and different sins, we find the rules upon the subject permeated by a spirit of discrimination between castes, classes and sexes. One is also struck by the emphasis laid on

[1] *Manu*, XI, 228-234.

trivial things, on mere matters of ritual or ceremonial and by the utter lack of any sense of proportion between the various offences for which penances are prescribed and between the character of the offences and the burden of the penances. I will now refer to some of the provisions of the law of penances as laid down in the Smṛtis. According to Manu, a false claim of high birth is equal in guilt to the slaying of a Brāhmaṇa; forgetting the Veda, giving false evidence, the eating of forbidden food and slaying a friend are considered equal to the drinking of spirituous liquor.[1] The list of Upapātakas (minor degrading sins) includes in the same category allowing a younger brother to marry before the elder, adultery, the sale of oneself, wife or child, defilement of a maiden, usury, breaking a vow, the sale of a tank or garden, teaching the Veda for a salary, learning the Veda from a paid teacher, selling goods which one ought not to sell, the superintendence of mines or factories, the execution of great engineering works, civil or mechanical, doing things for one's own good only, studying bad books, dancing and singing, revilement of the Vedas and the murder of women, Śūdras, Vaiśyas and Kṣattriyas.[2] The list of sins which caused loss of caste includes in the same category giving pain to a Brāhmaṇa by a blow, smelling at things which ought not to be smelt or at spirituous liquor, cheating and unnatural

[1] *Manu*, XI, 56-57.
[2] *Ibid.*, XI, 60-67.

offences with a human being.[1] A student who has broken his vow of chastity has to offer at night on a crossway to Nirṛti (the goddess of sin) an one-eyed ass, according to the rule for Pākayajñas. He has to go begging to seven houses, dressed in the hide of the ass, proclaiming his deed. Subsisting on a single daily meal by alms obtained there and bathing thrice a day, he becomes pure after the lapse of one year.[2] One-fourth of the penances for the murder of a Brāhmaṇa is prescribed as expiation for the killing of a Kṣattriya, one-eighth for killing a Vaiśya and one-sixteenth for killing a virtuous Śūdra.[3] He who has slain a Śūdra must perform the penance prescribed for the murder of a Brāhmaṇa during six months, or he may also give ten white cows and one bull to a Brāhmaṇa.[4] Having killed a cat, an ichneumon, a blue jay, a frog, a dog, an iguana, an owl or a crow, one must perform the penance for the murder of a Śūdra, or subsist on milk only during three days or walk hundred Yojanas or bathe in a river, or mutter a hymn addressed to the waters. For killing a snake, a Brāhmaṇa shall give a spade of black iron, for killing a eunuch, a load of straw and a Māṣa of lead.[5] For killing carnivorous wild beasts the offender should give a milch cow to a Brāhmaṇa.[6] For killing adulterous women of the

[1] *Manu*, XI, 68.
[2] *Ibid.*, XI, 119, 123, 124.
[3] *Ibid.*, XI, 127.
[4] *Ibid.*, XI, 131.
[5] *Ibid.*, XI, 132-134.
[6] *Ibid.*, XI, 138.

four castes, one must give, in order to purify oneself, a leathern bag, a bow, a goat, or a sheep respectively.[1] According to Gautama, no penance is necessary for killing a harlot.[2] A man who is asleep when the sun rises must remain standing during the day, continent and fasting; and one who is asleep when the sun sets must remain standing during the night, reciting the Gāyatrī.[3]

Sanātana Dharma.

While there are numerous dicta in our sacred literature laying down particular rules of conduct as rules of Sanātana Dharma, the term 'Sanātana Dharma' has not, so far as I know, been applied to the Dharma Śāstras collectively. I do not wish to suggest that there is any impropriety in applying the term 'Sanātana Dharma' to the entire collection of rules of conduct which have been individually called rules of Sanātana Dharma. The name was adopted by the authors of the elementary and advanced text-books on Hindu religion and ethics published by the Board of Trustees of the Central Hindu College at Benares about thirty years ago. It was used to indicate the eternal principles of religion and conduct considered to be the fundamental truths of Hinduism. The term has largely come into use in Hindu revivalist circles and an appeal is made to Sanātana Dharma for the purpose of resisting changes in the Hindu law. It is con-

[1] *Manu*, XI, 139.
[2] *Gautama*, XXII, 27.
[3] *Ibid.*, XXIII, 21.

tended that the rules contained in the Dharma Śāstras are eternal and immutable and not subject to alteration. The claim seems to be made on behalf of the whole body of the Dharma Śāstra and not with reference to any particular rules. If it is with reference to any particular rules, the champions of Sanātana Dharma have not explained which of them are, in their opinion, of eternal validity. So far as the orthodox view of the Dharma Śāstra is concerned, it may be taken that the claim of eternal validity covers the whole body of the Dharma Śāstra. But the brief survey we have made of the history of the most important topics comprised in the Dharma Śāstra will convince any unbiassed person that the rules of conduct and the ethical ideals underlying them have undergone great changes from time to time in accordance with social needs or changes of public opinion. The changes have in some cases been of a progressive character and in other cases of a reactionary or injurious tendency. But whatever may be the character of the changes in particular instances, the claim that the entire body of the Dharma Śāstra is eternal and immutable cannot be maintained. How many of the rules prescribed therein are unsuitable, impracticable and opposed to modern notions and conditions has been made abundantly clear in the course of the preceding chapters. Even the most ardent champions of Sanātana Dharma must shrink from any proposal to enforce the entire body of rules contained in the Smṛtis.

CHAPTER IX

DOCTRINE OF KARMA

THE doctrine of Karma, with the allied doctrine of Saṁsāra or re-birth, is one of the essential tenets of the Hindu religion and has profoundly influenced Hindu thought and life. It is deeply rooted in the minds of orthodox Hindus of all classes and grades. It has permeated Hindu philosophy, literature and art. The widespread belief in this doctrine has been noticed by every foreign observer and it has been so largely the subject of ill-informed and unfair criticism that it is necessary to explain its true import and its implications and consequences. The doctrine of Karma is based upon the following beliefs and assumptions:—

(1) that every act or deed must necessarily be followed by its consequences which are not merely of a physical character, but also mental and moral. It produces an effect upon the character, disposition, instincts and tendencies of the agent. The word Saṁskāra or Vāsanā indicates the physical, mental and moral traits with which a person is imbued and which emanate from previous experiences or actions. They form part of his personality and are borne by him in his lifetime and carried into a future existence;

(2) that the consequences of a person's acts not being fully worked out in this life, they demand a future life for their fruition;

(3) that the inequalities between men in worldly position and advantages and the apparent discord between their characters and their happiness or sufferings, their good or ill-fortune, conflict with our sense of justice and our conception of the benevolence of God and call for an explanation compatible with the moral government of the universe;

(4) that the doctrine of the immortality of the soul which justifies the belief in a future existence of the individual soul equally justifies its pre-existence; and

(5) that, while the happiness or suffering of a person in this life may not always be due to his own good or evil deeds in a prior birth, but may be due to the operation of circumstances beyond his control, or his actions in the present birth, the possibility of his own good or ill desert in a previous birth as the cause cannot be ruled out.

That the doctrine of Karma is not successful in solving all the problems of good or evil and good or bad fortune may be conceded. That it is more than a theory cannot be asserted or proved. But many of our most deeply rooted and widely held religious beliefs are equally incapable of proof. It may be fairly claimed by those who believe in the doctrine of Karma that it affords at least as satisfactory a basis for morality, if not a more satisfactory one, and is more consistent than other systems with our conception of the goodness and benevolence of God.[1] What has probably led to the violent dislike of the Christian to the doctrine of Karma is its implication or corollary of re-birth and transmigration of souls. While the Christian declares his belief in the immortality of the soul and in a life eternal, he is not prepared to carry his belief to its logical consequences or push his inquiries into the question of the pre-existence of the soul or the condition of the soul after this life. The idea of a special creation of each soul at the time of the birth of an individual is repugnant to the scientific spirit and really inconsistent with the doctrine of the immortality of the soul. To the Hindu, immortality is as much incompatible with creation at birth as with destruction at death. What is eternal cannot be born, in the sense that it comes into existence out of nothing. The theory of creation of something not previously existent is irreconcilable with anything of an eternal character and is logically inconceivable. Whether the conception of an endless succession of births and deaths is an inevitable corollary of the doctrine of Karma may be open to doubt. So far as the Hindu is concerned, he has a loophole of escape from the endless wheel of existence; he may obtain deliverance by true knowledge. The conception of an eternal life of rest or of restless activity may be equally unwelcome to certain classes of minds.

[1] For a discussion of the ethical difficulties common to all forms of monotheism, *see* L. T. Hobhouse: *Morals in Evolution*, Vol. II, Chapter IV, Sections 3 to 6.

If the soul of a man existed before his birth, where and in what form did it exist? It may be said that these are questions to which it is impossible to obtain an answer and that it is therefore idle to waste any time in seeking a solution of insoluble mysteries. Humanity is not content to give up the quest for light into the mysteries of life and death and the Hindu mind has been pertinaciously devoting itself to the solution of such riddles and has sought to discover an answer in speculative theories. From a rational point of view the tests to be applied to these theories are whether they furnish an intelligible and consistent answer to our questionings, whether they fit in coherently with the framework of our other beliefs, whether the implications or deductions of the theory are compatible with the claims of morality or social progress and whether it is more or less open to serious criticism than rival doctrines or other articles of religious faith. It may be confessed that the tests here proposed savour of a pragmatical character. But it is all that can be suggested from a rational point of view. Tried by these tests, the doctrine of Karma is acceptable to the Hindu mind as giving a much less unsatisfactory answer to the riddles of existence than other dogmas. Further speculation may suggest a partial modification of the doctrine or the rejection of some of its implications or corollaries. But there is no reason to reject the doctrine as intrinsically absurd, unreasonable or pernicious. On the other hand, the merits of the doctrine sustain a reasonable claim to belief. I am tempted here to quote a beautiful passage from Rhys Davids' Hibbert Lectures on *Indian Buddhism*: "The fact underlying all these theories (pre-destination, pre-existence, etc.) is acknowledged to be a very real one. The history of the individual does not begin with his birth. He has been endless generations in the making. And he cannot sever himself from his surroundings; no, not for an hour. The tiny snowdrop droops its fairy head just so much and no more, because it is balanced by the universe. It is a snowdrop, not an oak, and just that kind of snowdrop, because it is the outcome of the Karma of an endless series of past existences; and because it did not begin to be when the flower opened, or when the mother-plant first peeped above the ground, or first met the embraces of the sun, or when the bulb began to shoot beneath the soil, or at any time which you or I can fix. A great American writer says: 'It was a poetic attempt to lift this mountain of Fate, to reconcile this despotism of race with liberty, when the Hindoos said, Fate is nothing but the deeds committed in a prior state of existence.' I find the coincidence of Eastern and Western speculation in the daring statement of the German philosopher, Schelling, 'There is in every man a certain feeling that he has been what he is from all eternity.' We may put a new and deeper meaning into the words of the poet:

'. . . Our deeds follow us from afar,
And what we have been makes us what we are.'"[1]

We may now proceed to consider some of the objections which have been put forward by Christian missionaries and European scholars against this doctrine. One objection which has been commonly urged against this doctrine of Karma is that it leads to fatalism and paralyses human effort. That fatalism is inimical to moral progress, or for the matter of that, to any kind of progress may be readily granted. But it is an entire misconception of the doctrine of Karma to confound it with fatalism. The doctrine that what a man soweth he shall reap cannot be regarded as fatalism. The doctrine is no more open to the charge of fatalism than the theory of determinism or belief in the law of causation. Notwithstanding its hoary antiquity, the free will controversy still remains unsettled. After a careful examination, Sidgwick arrived at the conclusion that for the general regulation of conduct it is not practically important to decide the metaphysical question at issue in the free will controversy. Most people will be disinclined to enter the bog of metaphysical speculation to which this controversy has led. The Karma theory implies that a man can by his own actions influence his future destiny. The freedom of the individual to regulate his conduct by his own rational volitions and his ability to conquer his own impulses or other obstacles have always been emphasised in the

[1] Rhys Davids: *Indian Buddhism*, pp. 114-115.

clearest terms by the Hindu sages and law-givers. Far from undermining the foundations of moral responsibility, the doctrine of Karma strengthens them. The sacred literature of India has always recognised the importance of Puruṣakāra or human effort as essential to success in life. There are passages no doubt which also refer to the co-operation of other factors of success or failure, to the weight and influence of external conditions and internal tendencies and impulses which a man has to contend against and overcome. The sage Yājñavalkya laid down that the fruition of an act depended upon human effort and the favourable factors created by a man's own previous actions.[1] The Sūtrabhāṣya of Śaṅkara[2] exonerates God from the charge of partiality and cruelty by pointing out that rewards and punishments are awarded by Him in accordance with good or ill desert, and not arbitrarily, and that good or bad fortune is primarily dependent upon a man's own actions and efforts. It points out also that injunctions would be meaningless, if there were no freedom of action. Though there are some passages in the *Gītā* which refer to the overmastering influence of inherited tendencies and impulses which constitute a man's Prakṛti or nature, Arjuna is exhorted to conquer his passions and impulses and perform his appointed duty. For instance, in Ślokas 59 and 60 of Chapter XVIII of the *Gītā*, Śrī Kṛṣṇa refers to the overmastering tendency of his

[1] *Yājñavalkya,* I, 349, 351.
[2] II, iii, 42.

martial instinct as a Kṣattriya which would induce him to fight in spite of his foolish resolution not to fight. Śloka 61 refers to the Almighty who is seated in the hearts of all His creatures and is the origin of all their activities and is the universal background. Reading these passages along with other passages in the *Gītā* and with the exhortation to Arjuna in the beginning and end of the work to discharge his duty as a warrior and do battle in spite of his own inclinations, it would be an unreasonable interpretation to suggest that Śrī Kṛṣṇa denies the freedom of the will or Arjuna's ability to make a deliberate choice as between alternative courses. Śloka 63 makes this perfectly clear. It is strange that an eminent Sanskrit scholar like Prof. Keith should regard the conception of Karma as essentially fatalistic and as not furnishing for a moral mind a good incentive to moral progress.[1] It is equally strange that Prof. Keith should think that the Hindu doctrine of the Absolute as all-pervading involves the negation of human responsibility.[2] The metaphysical conception of the One and the Absolute in the transcendent plane has no bearing upon the relations of human beings in the phenomenal or empirical world which proceeds on the assumption not merely of duality, but of plurality and diversity. Hinduism imposes no greater burden upon the belief of its followers than any other system of religion which accepts an omni-

[1] A. B. Keith: *The Religion and Philosophy of the Veda and Upaniṣads*, p. 596.

[2] *Ibid.*, p. 586.

potent God as the creator of the universe. Every system of religion is driven to accept in the last resort a limited number of inconsistent and irreconcilable dogmas. If God is the creator of the whole universe, He can be also credited with the power of endowing man with freedom of the will. The word 'Niyati' or fate or destiny is no doubt used in many passages in our sacred books and literature; but it simply means the aggregate of the external factors or conditions which work either in a man's favour or against him. Human effort is not always attended with success; it requires the co-operation of several factors. The factors which are not dependent upon a man's own volition and which are arrayed against him, the circumstances which are beyond his control and could not have been foreseen and which go by the name of chance are called destiny or fate. Chance and destiny are respectively called in Sanskrit यदृच्छा and नियति and a contrast is often imagined between them. What happens by chance is as much bound to occur and is the result of causation as what happens by destiny. Destiny is merely an emphatic affirmation of causation.

The whole doctrine of Karma proceeds upon the postulate of human freedom and urges a man to rely upon himself and his own exertions instead of depending upon others and does not encourage an attitude of passivity or inaction. But when a man has striven and failed or has met with some unaccountable misfortune, he is consoled by the reflection that his failure or misfortune has been brought about by himself. "If we suffer, as most people do, from imperfections and misfortunes, it would be consoling to believe that these were punishments of our own acts in the past, not mere effects of the acts of other people, or of an indifferent nature over which we have no control. The world, I think, on this hypothesis would at least seem juster than it does on the positivist view, and that in itself would be a great gain."[1] He does not seek to throw the blame upon others or upon a capricious Supreme Being, and it rests with him so to exert himself as to deserve better success in the future. The Hindu does not believe in predestination irrespective of his own good or ill desert.

I have remarked above that the theory of Karma and Saṁsāra is not free from difficulties and perplexities of its own. It may be said that though the doctrine of Karma professes to explain the origin of evil and suffering, it does not really do so, inasmuch as it involves an infinite regression, as expressed in the doctrine that Karma is Anādi, a term which means that which has no ascertainable beginning in time. There are certain inexplicable ultimate postulates in the Hindu religion of which Karma is one. The other things which have no ascertainable beginning or are included in the Anādi category are जीव (individual soul), ईश्वर (God or Supreme Being), विशुद्धा चित् (the pure intelligence which is the underlying spirit or soul

[1] G. L. Dickinson: *Is Immortality Desirable*, pp. 40-41.

of the whole universe), जीवेशभेदः (the phenomenal distinction between the individual soul and God), अविद्या (nescience) and अविद्याचितोः संबन्धः (connection between Cit or pure intelligence and nescience).[1] The difference between these categories of Anādi and Karma is that the former are essentially without a beginning, while the latter is without a beginning in the sense that the succession or stream of action has no beginning. The doctrine of Karma is a more acceptable theory for staving off responsibility from the Creator for evil and suffering than any of the rival doctrines of other religions.

The theory of Saṁsāra is crossed and complicated by the theory of heaven and hell. Latter-day thinkers have endeavoured to reconcile the theories by suggesting that a man passes after death to other worlds of bliss or suffering and after a certain time returns to this world and is born again. The true explanation seems to me to be that the theory of heaven and hell which is a part of nearly all primitive creeds was also a feature of the ancient Hindu religion. But when people learned to believe in the law of causation and in the continuation of life and personality and were impelled to seek an explanation of the inequalities of status, fortune and happiness or suffering which would not impute arbitrariness, partiality or cruelty to God, they discovered an explanation in a man's

[1] जीव ईशो विशुद्धा चित् तथा जीवेशयोर्भिदा।
अविद्या तच्चितोर्योगः षडस्माकमनादयः ॥

Quoted by Acyutakrṣṇānanda in his commentary on the *Siddhāntaleśa Saṅgraha* (Kumbakonam edition), p. 305.

own actions in a previous birth. When they found that good or evil deeds did not always bring their rewards or punishments in this life, it was only a short step to the belief that actions in this life were bound to bear fruit in another birth. The demands of logical reasoning did not require a journey to another world and a return. But the texts which laid down the theory of heaven and hell stood and the unwillingness of the Hindu to admit the fallibility of the ancient scriptures or the obsolescence of old doctrines led him in this instance, as in many others, to make an elaborate attempt to reconcile irreconcilable texts by the introduction of an intermediate journey to another world and back.

Another conundrum which arises in connection with the theory of Karma is whether each good or bad action is bound to bear its fruit in due course or whether there can be an adjustment and set-off from time to time of good and bad deeds. There is no analogy in the processes of life which compels us to hold that the fruits or consequences of one deed cannot be counteracted or destroyed by another. As a matter of fact, certain penances and sacrifices and meritorious acts are supposed to have the effect of destroying the consequences of Karma.[1] But the general belief is against any such

[1] पापं चेत्पुरुषः कृत्वा कल्याणमभिपद्यते ।
मुच्यते सर्वपापेभ्यो महाभ्रेणेव चन्द्रमाः ॥
यथादित्यः समुद्यन्वै तमः पूर्वं व्यपोहति ।
एवं कल्याणमातिष्ठन् सर्वपापैः प्रमुच्यते ॥

Mahābhārata, Vanaparva, 207, 56-57.

adjustment or set-off in cases which do not come within the Śāstraic scheme of atonement.

Another difficulty raised by the theory of Karma is that while the effects of सञ्चितकर्म, *i.e.*, Karma which has accumulated and has not yet borne fruit, and वर्तमानकर्म, *i.e.*, actions in the present life, may be destroyed by knowledge of the Absolute, the effects of Prārabdhakarma which has begun to bear fruit in the present existence cannot be arrested and they must be fully worked out. This theory rests on the analogy of an arrow discharged from a bow which, it is said, cannot be arrested in its flight to its mark. There is no physical reason why an arrow or a bullet cannot be intercepted in its flight before it reaches its mark. The explanation probably is that as knowledge of the Supreme Being can be acquired during this existence, but is not immediately followed by deliverance from this mortal coil, a rationale has been invented in the theory of Prārabdhakarma, which requires a lifetime or more to work itself out.

The view that every action must produce effects upon one's physical, mental or moral constitution and that these effects may be inherited or carried over to the next birth is not hard to conceive. But why good and bad actions should be followed by prosperity or adversity in another birth is difficult to understand, unless we bring in the theory of retributive justice administered by God.

The theory of Karma involves the carrying over of character, instincts and tendencies to another birth. How far such inheritance is compatible with the laws of heredity so far as they have been ascertained is a question which it is not possible for laymen to answer. That the physical or corporeal lineage of every human being goes back to an indefinite, if not infinite, number of generations and that the germ-cell is practically immortal are generally admitted. That the mental and moral faculties and characteristics of an individual are also traceable to those of his corporeal ancestors is accepted as supported by observed facts. That there could be any spiritual lineage as involved in the theory of transmigration of souls apart from the corporeal lineage is a matter which is not demonstrable by any scientific method. If such a spiritual lineage or continuity of the soul or Jīva could be accepted, how such a theory could fit in with the accepted theory of heredity it is not possible to explain. But the Hindus believe that certain phenomena like the sudden appearance of a genius and certain emotional experiences, longings and propensities which seem unaccountable by any definable and definite causes according to the materialistic theory of evolution may be more easily accounted for by the theory of the continuity of the individual soul and its experiences in former lives during the course of its evolution. The question is whether there is anything like an evolution of the soul as distinguished from the evolution of the body with the necessary mental and moral concomitants. The theory of heredity, so far as established, does not seem to be altogether sufficient. Is the other theory admissible to supplement it? It is perhaps possible to suggest that in the course of its wanderings or evolution the Jīva chooses such corporeal conditions in the shape of parentage as may be favourable to its development or suitable to its aptitudes and characteristics. These speculations into the mysteries of life, birth and heredity can only obtain arbitrary, fanciful, or mystic solutions. If the utterances of gifted poets are attributable to a deeper vision into the inwardness of things, there may be truth in the observation of Kālidāsa that "if when in the midst of happiness the mind is perturbed at the sight of beautiful things or the hearing of sweet sounds, it must surely be due to a vague reminiscence of loves or friendships in a previous birth which have left an indelible impress on the soul."[1]

We may now proceed to notice some of the other objections which have been urged against the doctrine of Karma. Several of these objections are mutually contradictory. It has been said that according to the doctrine of Karma we cannot justify the admiration of pain and suffering endured by men for the sake of others, or the relief of suffering which is the result of a man's own deeds. It has been already pointed out that the doctrine of Karma is an emphatic affirmation and

[1] 'रम्याणि वीक्ष्य मधुरांश्च निशम्य शब्दान्
पर्युत्सुको भवति यत्सुखितोऽपि जन्तुः ।
तच्चेतसा स्मरति नूनमबोधपूर्वं
भावस्थिराणि जननान्तरसौहृदानि ॥'

Śākuntala, V, 2.

vindication of the freedom of the human will. It does not therefore prevent a man's deliberate choice of suffering for the sake of others. Nor does the doctrine affirm that all suffering, voluntary or involuntary, must be the result of actions in a previous birth. Nor again does the doctrine prevent a man from acting in accordance with his reason and the dictates of humanity. Even if a person's suffering were the result of his own past misdeeds, there is no reason why a spectator should leave him to his sufferings and not minister to his relief. The idea that a man is under a moral obligation not to relieve another from the natural consequences of his former deeds finds no support in the theory of Karma or in the Hindu scriptures and it is a gross libel on the Hindu community to say that it is callous to suffering.

CHAPTER X

SOME FUNDAMENTAL QUESTIONS

The Moral Standard

THE tendency of ethical speculation has been to shift the moral standard from an external source to an internal one. Except in later Greece, society in ancient times was generally disposed to seek the authority of moral rules in law, religion and social opinion. The Hindu system of ethics was no exception to this general rule. It has been already pointed out in the introductory chapter that ancient Hindu thought preferred to lay the foundations of morality in the scriptures, in the example of the virtuous and learned, and, failing these, in one's own conscience. It is only when the external standards were silent or when there was any doubt or difficulty in the application of the rules derived from such external standards that a resort to the dictates of conscience or one's own moral sense or judgment was allowed.

The ideas of duty, happiness and perfection have not been subjected in Hindu thought to the same severe analysis and examination as in western systems of ethics. But the question of the ends of human action occupies a large place in our system of ethics. In spite of all their elaborate discussion and investigation, no agreement has yet been reached on these points by western ethical thinkers. Volumes have been written about the claims of happiness or perfection to be regarded as the *summum bonum*. But the advocates of neither view have been able to convince the advocates of the other. So far as the ordinary rules of morality are concerned, there is no serious difference between the different schools. The disputes relate to the theoretical foundations of the accepted rules of moral conduct. The value of the discussions consists in the satisfaction afforded by the discovery of a rational basis of conduct for our ethical judgments and in the light that may be thrown by the theory in cases of conflict and doubt or the line of future advance.

Puruṣārthas or ends of Conduct.

According to Hindu ethical thought, the ends of human action are four: Dharma (duty or virtue), Artha (wealth), Kāma (pleasure or happiness) and Mokṣa (salvation or emancipation). Of these four objects of human endeavour Dharma and Artha are not primary ends, or ends in themselves, but are means to the other two ends, Kāma and Mokṣa. Kāma and Mokṣa are not means to other ends, but are regarded as ultimate ends. As between the two, Mokṣa is undoubtedly regarded as the *summum bonum* or the highest end. But what is the conception of Mokṣa? According to the Advaita Vedāntin, it is a condition which not merely involves the extinction of all suffering and unhappiness, but is also a positive state of supreme and unalloyed bliss. It is a result of self-realisation, of the identification of the self with the spirit of the whole universe. The term 'Kāma' is used to denote विषयानुभवजन्यसुख, *i.e.*, pleasures or happiness derived from contact with the external objects of sense or the sources of intellectual or emotional satisfaction.[1] The word 'Kāma' would include not merely the pleasures of the senses, but also all pleasures derived from the exercise of the mental faculties. It would include the pleasures of the aesthetic faculty also. Strictly speaking, pleasures and happiness all connote desirable states of conscious existence. But in the phraseology of ethical writers a distinction is often drawn between happiness and pleasure. There is a prejudice against the use of the term 'pleasure' which in ordinary English usage suggests too prominently the coarser and commoner kinds of pleasures which involve as concomitant or consequent either a greater amount of pain or a loss of more important pleasures.[2] Similarly the word 'Kāma' is often popularly used to signify the coarser pleasures of the senses and the word has attracted the same prejudice as the English word 'pleasures'. The Sanskrit word सुख or आनन्द has no such implications and is used generically to denote any state of desirable conscious existence or experience. The

[1] इन्द्रियाणां च पञ्चानां मनसो हृदयस्य च ।
विषये वर्तमानानां या प्रीतिरुपजायते ॥
स काम इति मे बुद्धिः कर्मणां फलमुत्तमम् ।

Mahābhārata, Vanaparva, 33, 37-38.

[2] *See* H. Sidgwick: *Methods of Ethics*, p. 402.

difference between Kāma and Mokṣa is that while both imply happiness, Kāma is a limited and measurable condition, while Mokṣa denotes a state of unbounded and immeasurable felicity. As the true nature and essence of the Ātman is supreme bliss and intelligence, one who realises the true nature of the Self or Ātman realises a condition of blissfulness which requires no contact with any external objects and is independent of all external means, causes or occasions. It is not quite easy to identify the Hindu theory of the *summum bonum* exclusively with any of the theories which adopt happiness, perfection or self-realisation as the ultimate end. In so far as the condition of the emancipated soul is described as one of ineffable bliss, it may be held that happiness is the ultimate end adopted in Hindu ethics. But in so far, however, as emancipation requires a severe and arduous course of moral discipline, the control of the lower elements of our human nature by the higher and the realisation of the true Self or Ātman, it may be equally correctly said that the *summum bonum* of the Hindus involves also perfection and self-realisation. The attainment of the *summum bonum,* though possible, is not within the reach of all. For all ordinary persons the other three ends of life are possible of attainment, and the bliss or happiness which they can obtain varies according to their capacity and merit. Though Kāma is a primary end and Dharma and Artha are only secondary ends, they are all closely inter-dependent. The pursuit of Kāma or

Artha by itself in contravention of Dharma or duty is forbidden. Wealth is desirable as a means to the performance of duty and the attainment of happiness.[1] Secondary ends often become primary and Dharma, though secondary to the ultimate end of Mokṣa, has acquired a predominance in relation to the other ends. The superiority of Dharma to the other two ends is emphasised in the *Rāmāyaṇa.*[2]

Though the three ends are thus closely dependent upon each other and the performance of Dharma or duty is inculcated as promoting the other ends also, the performance of duty for its own sake was enjoined in the later ethical writings. During Vedic times the performance of Dharma which included sacrifices and rituals was, in many cases, prompted by a desire for rewards in this world and in the next. The reward of Svarga which is held out in the Śrutis as the result of the performance of certain sacrificial rites and which is popularly known

[1] *Mahābhārata, Śāntiparva*, 167, 12-14.

[2] धर्मार्थकामा: किल तात लोके
समीक्षिता धर्मफलोदयेषु ।
ते तत्र सर्वे स्युरसंशयं मे
भार्येव वश्याभिमता सुपुत्रा ॥
यस्मिंस्तु सर्वे स्युरसंनिविष्टा
धर्मो यतः स्यात्तदुपक्रमेत ।
द्वेष्यो भवत्यर्थपरो हि लोके
कामात्मता खल्वपि न प्रशस्ता ॥

Rāmāyaṇa, Ayodhyākāṇḍa, 21, 57-58.

See also:—

धर्माविरुद्धो भूतेषु कामोऽस्मि भरतर्षभ ॥

Bhagavadgītā, VII, 11.

as heaven is interpreted by the Mīmāṁsaka as unalloyed felicity.[1]

Though Mokṣa is ordinarily held to be attainable only after death, it is also regarded as possible, though but extremely rarely, of attainment in this life. For instance, the king Janaka and the sage Vyāsa are believed to have attained emancipation during their mundane existence. A person who has attained to a true knowledge of the Ātman and to the realisation of the Self by identifying himself with the spirit or soul of the universe transcends the plane of ordinary moral life, having already, by his moral discipline and spiritual knowledge, shed all his sins. Though bound by no earthly ties, the Jīvanmukta devotes the remaining days of his earthly existence to the guidance and spiritual enlightenment of humanity. This task of guidance and enlightenment of other persons he undertakes not under any sense of obligation, but of his own free will and accord. That such persons devote themselves to this kind of work is an inference from the text of the Śruti आचार्यवान् पुरुषो वेद.[2] They devote themselves also to the cultivation of Bhakti, to the selfless adoration and contemplation of the Supreme Being.[3]

[1] यन्न दुःखेन संभिन्नं न च ग्रस्तमनन्तरम् ।
अभिलाषोपनीतं च तत्सुखं स्वःपदास्पदम् ॥

That condition of happiness which is unmixed with pain or sorrow and is lasting and is an object of desire.

[2] *Chāndogyopaniṣad*, VI, xiv, 2.

[3] आत्मारामाश्च मुनयो निर्ग्रन्था अप्युरुक्रमे ।
कुर्वन्त्यहैतुकीं भक्तिमित्थंभूतगुणो हरिः ॥

Śrīmad Bhāgavatam, I, vii, 10.

The four Āśramas and the ways of salvation.

The pursuit of Mokṣa as the *summum bonum* is generally held to require Saṁnyāsa or renunciation of the world as a means and preparation. But ordinarily a person is not expected to enter upon the Āśrama (or order of life) of a Saṁnyāsin, until he has discharged his duties in the three previous orders of life. The theory of the four Āśramas or stages of life is closely connected with the question of moral ends or Puruṣārthas. The first Āśrama is that of the Brahmacārin or student, the second is that of the Gṛhastha or householder and the third that of the Vānaprastha or anchorite. It is only by passing through these stages that a twice-born man can ordinarily discharge his duties to the world. In the Upaniṣads, an option is given to a man to enter upon the Āśrama of a Saṁnyāsin from any of the three other Āśramas, the only condition being that he should be a विरक्त (free from attachment to the world). But Manu, who took a more common-sense view of the duties of men, condemned the pursuit of Mokṣa without previously discharging one's duties to the world.[1] It may also be said that the view put forward by Manu of the successive adoption of the Āśramas is more in accordance with the natural course of man's life, according to which the first part is devoted to his education, the second to the pursuit of wealth by the exercise of some lawful calling or occupation and the fulfilment of one's duties to society, and the third to retirement from active life and the adop-

[1] *Manu*, VI, 35.

tion of the life of a recluse in the forest with a view to the practice of religious meditation and austerities. Though every twice-born man is bound to go through the first stage of a student, it is, according to the Upaniṣads, not obligatory to pass through any of the other three stages. The householder's order of life is considered by Manu to be the most important and responsible of all, for the members of the other three orders of life are supported by the householder and are dependent upon him for their learning and sustenance. The responsibilities of that order require the due control of the senses for their proper discharge.[1] The spiritual insight which is essential to salvation may be acquired either by the path of Jñāna (knowledge), or by the performance of Karma (duty) or by Bhakti (faith). Renunciation of the world or Nivṛtti is not an essential condition of salvation. The performance of duty for the sake of duty is also considered to be Nivṛtti (renunciation) and has the same efficacy.[2]

[1] यस्मात्त्रयोऽप्याश्रमिणो ज्ञानेनान्नेन चान्वहम् ।
गृहस्थेनैव धार्यन्ते तस्माज्ज्येष्ठाश्रमो गृही ॥
स संधार्यः प्रयत्नेन स्वर्गमक्षयमिच्छता ।
सुखं चेहेच्छता नित्यं योऽधार्यो दुर्बलेन्द्रियैः ॥

Manu, III, 78-79.

See also:—

धर्मेण चतुरो वर्णान् पालयन्क्लेशमाप्नुहि ।
चतुर्णामाश्रमाणां हि गार्हस्थ्यं श्रेष्ठमाश्रमम् ॥

Rāmāyaṇa, Ayodhyākāṇḍa, 106, 22.

[2] *Manu*, XII, 89-90; *Bhagavadgītā*, VI, 1.

The view of salvation entertained by the Hindus underwent a process of gradual evolution from the Vedic age to that of the *Gītā* and Manu. The original view was the attainment of happiness in heaven by the performance of religious rites. During this age, renunciation of the world was not insisted upon as a condition of salvation. During the age of the Upaniṣads the view that the world was full of sorrow and suffering took possession of thoughtful minds. Speculation on the mysteries of life and death and the problem of existence led to the development of the doctrine of Karma and Saṁsāra. This was the age which gave birth to the various systems of philosophy. The aim which these systems of philosophy set before themselves was the emancipation of the human soul from the bondage of Saṁsāra. It was during this age that the idea of Saṁnyāsa or renunciation of the world and retirement from the active duties of life acquired ascendancy over the minds of philosophers. The practical necessity of reconciling this view of salvation with the claims of the every-day world and of social life led to a reaction against the doctrine of renunciation as the indispensable means of obtaining Mokṣa. A solution was discovered in the *Gītā* and in *Manu* by which it was possible to accommodate the theory of emancipation to the demands of society and practical life. The solution adopted was that the performance of the duties imposed upon a person by his station in life or by his relations to his fellow-beings from a pure sense of duty and without any motive of reward (निष्कामकर्म) afforded the same means and opportunities of spiritual development as Saṁnyāsa and was equally efficacious for the attainment of the highest end. The ideal emphasised by the *Gītā* is a life of action and not of passivity or repose. What stands in the way of salvation is not activity or response to the demands of life and society, but undue attachment to the ends of the world. The attitude of mind which the *Gītā* again and again inculcates is the temper of stoicism. Though numberless commentaries have been written on the *Gītā*, its teaching requires to be interpreted afresh in the light of the new forms and conditions of society and the demands made upon the individual by his own surroundings and situations and in the light of modern knowledge. This has been the case with other great religions also and notably with Christianity. The modernist view of the Gospels is far removed from that of the primitive church or even the interpretation of the last century. When the *Gītā* speaks of the control of the senses and of looking with indifference upon pleasures and pains, it would be irrational to suggest that what the *Gītā* recommends is that we should cultivate an attitude of insensibility to pleasures and pains; it only means that we should abstain from cultivating excessive attachment to the pleasures of the senses. Similarly the *Gītā* does not teach that we should not be susceptible to the kindly feelings and instincts of humanity, to the emotions of love, compassion, benevolence, charity, etc. Mastery of reason and judgment over the emotions and not the mastery of the latter over the former, serenity and poise of mind and the discharge of duty without an eye to personal advantage or rewards are the essence of the teaching of the *Gītā*. What is enjoined is not inability to perceive or appreciate differences of experience, but freedom from undue attachment to them. The metaphysical doctrine of the unity of the soul or Atman with the Paramātman or the Supreme Being or the spirit of the universe and the teaching that the realisation of this unity is the supreme end and aim of human beings afford the strongest foundation and incentive for a system of lofty morality.

Conception of duty.

The notion of duty or obligation has undergone the most critical examination and analysis at the hands of European thinkers. Many of them have confessed that it is impossible to give any satisfactory analysis or definition of the notion of duty. There is a repugnance on the part of many thinkers, especially of the intuitionist school, to explain it on any hedonistic basis. Duty and interest do not always coincide, and where they do not, the problem of accounting for the sense of duty is attended with difficulties. The reconciliation between duty and interest is effected by theologians by the hypothesis of sanctions in a future life. Modern ethical writers are inclined to take the view that such sanctions seriously detract from the merit of a virtuous character or action. But even those who take this view consider it quite possible to reconcile the disinterested performance of duty with the theory of the beatific consequences of virtue. It is sometimes said by theologians that while a virtuous life will bear fruit in the shape of beatitude in a future existence, such beatitude should not operate as a motive for virtuous acts or a virtuous life. Psychologically there is a distinction between intention and motive; the former implies a knowledge of the consequences, the latter involves a desire to reap those consequences. Honesty, for instance, may be the best policy, but a person who acts honestly may do so entirely from a sense of duty and without any desire for the reputation of honesty or for any of the incidental advantages which may flow from such a reputation. It would be unreasonable to suggest that unless an honest person is ignorant of the incidental consequences and advantages, he cannot be regarded as having acted from a sense of duty. Marks of honour and distinction are bestowed upon those who have distinguished themselves by their bravery and heroism. But these do not operate as the motives to acts of supreme bravery or self-sacrifice. In the same way mere knowledge of future consequences in the shape of beatitude cannot be held to be a taint in the character, actions or life of a virtuous man, unless he is actuated by a desire for such advantages. The psychological distinction between the two states of mind may appear to be subtle. Nevertheless their existence must be conceded and the distinction is real. Theologians and moralists who consider it essential to effect a reconciliation between duty and interest imply that interest furnishes the motive for the performance of duty, or that the moral government of the world is defective and that the balance has to be redressed in a future world. If men could be expected to perform their duties without any knowledge of personal advantage or even with a certain knowledge of personal disadvantage or sacrifice, there would be no reason or necessity for theological sanctions except in the interests of poetic justice. It may perhaps be urged that while such sanctions are unnecessary in the case of those who have a natural inclination to virtue, they would be necessary in the case of those who are morally weak or undisciplined.

The meaning of the imperative has undergone examination at the hands of the Sanskrit grammarians and logicians. According to them it involves three elements: (1) इष्टसाधनताज्ञान (the knowledge of the act being the means to a desirable end), (2) बलवदनिष्टाननुबन्धित्वज्ञान (the knowledge that the act will not be followed by more harm than good), and (3) कृतिसाध्यताज्ञान (the knowledge that the act is feasible). This view has been generally adopted by the Naiyāyikas and corresponds to the theory of psychological hedonism, and it may be said that it does not recognise the existence of a sense of obligation divorced from the interest of the agent. But it may be urged that it only contemplates the ultimate coincidence of duty and interest and that it does not preclude the fulfilment of duties without a desire for advantage.

Duty for its own sake.

The later ethical thought of the Hindus insists in the clearest and most emphatic terms upon the performance of duty for its own sake. "Your concern is with actions alone; never with their fruits. Let not the fruit of action be your motive. Let not inaction be your principle."[1] "Therefore always perform your duties, without regard for the fruits. He who does his duty without attachment attains the Supreme."[2] "That sacrifice is regarded as Sāttvika (proceeding from pure motives) which is performed without any desire of reward and solely from a sense of duty because it is prescribed by scripture."[3] Yudhiṣṭhira tells Draupadī, "I do not, O Princess, follow Dharma with an eye for reward. I give, simply because it is my duty to give; I sacrifice, because I must do so. Be there any reward or not, whatever must be per-

[1] कर्मण्येवाधिकारस्ते मा फलेषु कदाचन ।
मा कर्मफलहेतुर्भूर्मा ते सङ्गोऽस्त्वकर्मणि ॥
Bhagavadgītā, II, 47.

[2] तस्मादसक्तः सततं कार्यं कर्म समाचार ।
असक्तो ह्याचरन्कर्म परमाप्नोति पूरुषः ॥
Ibid., III, 19.

[3] अफलाकांक्षिभिर्यज्ञो विधिदृष्टो य इज्यते ।
यष्टव्यमेवेति मनः समाधाय स सात्त्विकः ॥
Ibid., XVII, 11.

formed by a householder, I do it, O Draupadī, according to my ability. O Draupadī with lovely hips, I practise Dharma with no regard to its fruits. I follow the scriptures and the example of good men. My mind is fixed upon Dharma for its own sake, O Draupadī, because it is naturally inclined to do so. He who practises Dharma for its rewards traffics in Dharma and is contemptible among those who talk of Dharma. He who wishes to extract advantages out of Dharma never acquires its real fruits."[1]

Whether the ultimately hedonistic character of religions is reconcilable or not with the theory of duty for the sake of duty, the Hindu system of ethics labours under no heavier difficulties than any other religion.

Adhikāribheda or Relativity.

It is a characteristic feature of Hinduism that it does not prescribe the same goal and method of

[1] नाहं धर्मफलाकाङ्क्षी राजपुत्रि चराम्युत ।
ददामि देयमित्येव यजे यष्टव्यमित्युत ॥
अस्तु वात्र फलं मा वा कर्तव्यं पुरुषेण यत् ।
गृहे निवसता कृष्णे यथाशक्ति करोमि तद् ॥
धर्मं चरामि सुश्रोणि न धर्मफलकारणात् ।
आगमाननतिक्रम्य सतां वृत्तमवेक्ष्य च ॥
धर्म एव मनः कृष्णे स्वभावाच्चैव मे धृतम् ।
धर्मवाणिज्यको हीनो जघन्यो धर्मवादिनाम् ॥
न धर्मफलमाप्नोति यो धर्मं दोग्धुमिच्छति ।

Mahābhārata, Vanaparva, 31, 2-6.

salvation for all persons irrespective of their capacity and their standard of spiritual development. A course of discipline and intellectual and spiritual training which may suit a more spiritually evolved person may not be practicable for another of inferior development. Karma, Bhakti and Jñana are different ways of salvation. The highest goal is one and the same and can only be reached by the path of spiritual knowledge which is hard and steep. Those who are engaged in the performance of works reach heaven. But their bliss is not eternal. Those who engage in Upāsanā or concentrated meditation of the Supreme Being in some aspect reach Brahmaloka by a different path. It is only those who acquire a true knowledge of the Brahman that attain emancipation.

CHAPTER XI

CHARGES AGAINST HINDU ETHICS AND ITS MERITS

We may now proceed to notice some of the charges against Hindu ethics made by Christian writers and see whether they are well founded. It is often stated that the Hindu religion is pessimistic and that pessimism cannot possibly furnish an adequate incentive to morality. Pessimism implies the conviction that evil and suffering predominate over good and happiness. In so far as he believes in another world, the Hindu believes in the possibility of attaining a supreme condition of happiness, even if it is denied to him in this world. Nor even so far as this world is concerned, can the Hindu be considered a pessimist. In the Ṛg Vedic times the Hindu prayed for length of days and prosperity in this life and for happiness in the next.[1] There are passages in some of the Upaniṣads which emphasise the sorrows and miseries of mundane existence, and there are numerous passages in the Purāṇas which dwell in great detail upon the evils and sufferings which fall to the lot of man in this world. But these passages must all be attributed to the habit of rhetorical exaggeration often resorted to by Hindu writers. To decry a thing for the purpose of praising another by way of

[1] A. B. Keith: *The Religion and Philosophy of the Veda and Upaniṣads*, p. 480.

contrast is a well-known figure of speech in Sanskrit known as व्याजस्तुति.[1] As Prof. Keith remarks, to find real pessimism in the Upaniṣads apart from mild expressions of the unsatisfactoriness of the finite compared with the infinite is impossible.[2] In Christianity and other religions also a feeling of dissatisfaction with this world is frequently expressed on the ground that it is full of misery and sorrow, and the pious Christian looks forward to another world for happiness. There seems no greater reason to attribute pessimism to the Hindu religion than to other systems. The real issue involved in this question is whether life in this world is worth living. Notwithstanding the expression of feelings of disappointment, despair or disgust with this world which humanity very often experiences and which is and must be reflected in the literature of every country, it is impossible to maintain that Hindus do not consider life on this planet to be worth living. The Hindus have been as capable of experiencing and appreciating the joys of life as any other nation. The great epic poems, the dramatic literature, the Dharma Śāstra, the Arthaśāstra and various other branches of literature all presuppose the desirability of life. The urge of life is so deep-rooted and imperious that it would be a wonder if any society were really pessimistic. Genuine pessimism is an impossibi-

[1] उक्तिर्व्याजस्तुतिर्निन्दास्तुतिभ्यां स्तुतिनिन्दयोः

Kuvalayānanda.

[2] A. B. Keith: *The Religion and Philosophy of the Veda and Upaniṣads*, p. 581.

lity and an absurdity, and can only be the result of a diseased mind or body. Some persons may have a pessimistic temperament and many may feel pessimistic at times. But it cannot possibly be an abiding feeling or conviction throughout life. The only logical course for a true pessimist would be suicide. It would be impossible for any society or nation to hold together or continue to exist, if its members believed in pessimism. The fact that no one wishes to shorten his life and that most people wish to prolong life if possible indicates the belief that they consider life to be worth living. Whether the belief is well founded or not is immaterial for our present purposes. Nor is it relevant to consider whether from an objective point of view the life lived or led by most people can be regarded as worthy and deserving of maintenance or prolongation. No society has shaped its code of conduct in the belief that life is not worth living. The conviction implied in the daily conduct of life is happily expressed by Vālmīki in the words he puts into the mouth of Sītā who says:

कल्याणी बत गाथेयं लौकिकी प्रतिभाति मे ।
एति जीवन्तमानन्दो नरं वर्षशतादपि ॥[1]

that it is a cheering adage that happiness comes to the living even after a hundred years. The religious teachers of mankind have often considered it necessary to dwell upon the sufferings of life on earth, upon the triviality and

[1] *Rāmāyaṇa, Sundarakāṇḍa*, 34, 6.

futility of the objects on which men set their hearts and upon the fleeting character of earthly pleasures and joys, for the purpose of weaning men from excessive attachment to temporal aims and attracting them to a spiritual life. But notwithstanding the gloomy pictures of earthly life drawn by the religious teacher and the philosopher, the world has gone on with its belief in the value of life. Dissatisfaction with the imperfections of our lot on earth or aspiration to a brighter and happier world does not amount to a negation of the value of life or of the worth-whileness of attempts to ameliorate and improve man's condition here. It has been remarked by a recent Christian writer that in Hindu thought the goal is represented as for most men so distant and the way to it as controlled by forces that are in a very real sense alien to most, that we feel justified in maintaining that Hindu thought is pessimistic in the extreme.[a] In reply we may quote the observation of another European writer that Indian thought does not really go much further than Christianity in pessimism; but its pessimism is intellectual rather than emotional. The charge of pessimism is applicable to Christian teaching. "Modern and mediæval Christianity—as witness many popular hymns—regards this world as vain and transitory, a vale of tears and tribulation, a troubled sea through whose way we must pass before we reach our rest. And choirs sing, though without much conviction, that it is weary waiting here. This language seems justified by

[a] J. McKenzie: *Hindu Ethics*, p. 216.

both the Gospels and the Epistles. Both Christ and St. Paul teach that the world is evil or at least spoiled and distorted."[1] It is sufficient for our purpose to repudiate the charge of pessimism brought against Hinduism. Whether it is necessary to go further and contend for an optimistic view of life is a different matter. It is too often the fashion for people to proclaim themselves optimists for the purpose of holding up their own spirits or their fellow-men's when plunged in adversity and despair, or for the purpose of putting forth effort for an improvement of their condition. Whether an optimistic view of the world and of its progress is justified or not is a question upon which some observations will be made later. It is sufficient here to remark that a declaration or spirit of optimism need not be regarded as a virtue and that whether a feeling of optimism is justifiable in any particular situation depends entirely upon the circumstances of the time. In the words of Dean Inge, "An optimist is a barometer stuck at Set Fair whatever the weather may be. The man who says 'I am always an optimist' is a very irritating kind of fool. He is the kind of man who would buy from a Jew and sell to a Scot and expect to make a profit."[2]

Another charge which has been brought against Hinduism is that it lays more stress upon

[1] Sir Charles Eliot: *Hinduism and Buddhism, Introduction*, p. lix.

[2] Dean Inge in *Points of View*, published by George Allen and Unwin, p. 48.

the negative virtues and upon a blameless life and inculcates a spirit of quietism as opposed to the strenuous pursuit of the aim of social service.[1] Max Müller remarked that "as a popular philosophy the Vedānta would have its dangers, that it would fail to call out and strengthen the manly qualities required for the practical side of life, and that it might raise the human mind to a height from which the most essential virtues of social and political life might dwindle away into mere phantoms."[2] There is no doubt that many of the virtues inculcated by Hinduism are of a negative character. But this is the case with other religions also. The same charge has been brought against Christianity. The Sermon on the Mount pronounces beatitudes upon the passive virtues rather than upon the active. Those who are blessed are the poor in spirit, the meek, the merciful, the pure in heart, the peacemakers, those who mourn, those who hunger and thirst after righteousness, those who are persecuted for the sake of righteousness and those who are reviled and persecuted. The virtues which are commended by Christ are the virtues of quietism and not the virtues of strenuous and active life. J. S. Mill remarked that the ideal of Christianity was negative rather than positive, passive rather than active, innocence rather than nobleness, abstinence from evil rather than active pursuit of good, and that in its precepts 'thou shalt not' predominates unduly over 'thou shalt'. Lecky remarks

[1] J. McKenzie: *Hindu Ethics*, pp. 208-209.

[2] F. Max Müller: *Six Systems of Indian Philosophy*, p. 253.

that while the eye of the pagan philosopher was ever fixed upon virtue, the eye of the Christian teacher was fixed upon sin.[1] "The change from the heroic to the saintly ideal, from the ideal of Paganism to the ideal of Christianity, was a change from a type which was essentially male to one which was essentially feminine."[2] "An ideal type in which meekness, gentleness, patience, humility, faith and love are the most prominent features, is not naturally male, but female."[3] "The relations of Christianity to the sentiment of patriotism were from the first very unfortunate."[4] "Patriotism itself as a duty has never found any place in Christian ethics and a strong theological feeling has usually been directly hostile to its growth. Ecclesiastics have no doubt taken a large share in political affairs, but this has been in most cases solely with the object of wresting them into conformity with ecclesiastical designs; and no other body of men have so uniformly sacrificed the interests of their country to the interests of their class."[5] The growth of the civic virtue of patriotism and, very much later in history, of the feeling of nationalism, in western countries is due not to the teaching of Christianity, but to various other causes to be sought in the political history of European countries. The political history of India on the other hand

[1] W. E. H. Lecky: *History of European Morals* (*Library edition*), Vol. II, p. 4.

[2] *Ibid.*, Vol. II, p. 383.

[3] *Ibid.*, Vol. II, p. 384.

[4] *Ibid.*, Vol. II, p. 149.

[5] *Ibid.*, Vol. II, p. 154.

has had an entirely different course. Geography, climate, food, race and other factors have also had their share in shaping the civic virtues of a nation. Loyalty to the established institutions and government, love of order and security have been the characteristics of the people of India. Love of freedom and adventure, a spirit of change and restlessness have been the characteristics of the European mentality. Yet it would be hazardous to lay down any sweeping general propositions. Kingdoms have from time immemorial existed in India and kings have made war upon neighbouring states and sent military expeditions to distant countries; and this could not have been done without the maintenance of armies or the promotion of the military spirit and the love of adventure and conquest. The virtues and martial instincts of the warrior and the joys of battle have not been less appreciated in India than in other countries. Lecky expressed the opinion that the moral influence of Christianity during the early period was more pronounced in the field of private life and upon individuals than in the sphere of civic and political life. It promoted individual self-culture, domestic morals and private charity rather than patriotism and public spirit.[1] Another modern writer remarks, "Christianity has no theory of society by which to guide itself. Its doctrine is personal."[2] "Amid all the wonderful descriptions of charity, of love, of self-surrender, we

[1] W. E. H. Lecky: *History of European Morals (Library edition)*, Vol. II, p. 156.

[2] L. T. Hobhouse: *Morals in Evolution*, Vol. II, p. 152.

hear very little of justice. Indeed how could it be otherwise? What need of justice when love readily yields up all? Why talk of a fair division to one who, if his cloak be taken, will make that a ground for giving up his garment? What need of equal rights among men who claim nothing for themselves and yield all they have to all who want? The code of the Sermon on the Mount appears to contemplate what in modern phrase we should call a voluntaryist or Anarchist community. Non-resistance is its central feature."[11] Apart from the fact that the charge brought against Hindu teaching is equally applicable to Christianity and other religions, there are various circumstances to account for the greater stress laid upon the quietistic virtues than upon those of strenuous social service. In the beginnings of social life in any country negative virtues are far more vital than the positive. The repression or suppression of lawless instincts, the control of unbridled selfishness and the harnessing of human nature to the requirements of social life and order require the observance and enforcement of the principle of justice and the penal code. However high the positive virtues may be in the scale of merit, the negative virtues are the indispensable foundation of any ordered system of society. The positive virtues of kindliness and sympathy towards fellow-beings, of help to the poor and the distressed, of hospitality, of charity and of love towards others come at a later stage and serve to promote and enrich social life. The idea of social service as now

[11] L. T. Hobhouse: *Morals in Evolution*, Vol. II, p. 152.

understood is a feature of modern times. As observed by Dean Inge with reference to early Christianity, there were no 'causes' in antiquity. The many humanitarian movements which have come into existence are of quite recent growth and it is not fair to set down the absence of such movements in earlier days to the fault of the ethical teaching of either Christianity or Hinduism or to trace their growth in the West to any special features and influence of Christianity.

In the next place, there are numerous passages in our sacred books in which stress is laid upon the virtues of disinterested performance of one's duty, compassion, kindness to all creatures, generosity, charity, hospitality, truthfulness, non-injury and returning good for evil. The golden rule of morality to treat others as oneself had been preached by Hinduism long before the Christian era. "He who has attained mental equipoise by steady meditation and who sees the Self or Atman in all beings and all beings in the Self or Atman realises the Brahman in all."[1] "I am never absent to him who sees me everywhere and finds everything in me. Nor is he ever absent to me."[2] "He who looks upon all like himself and treats their pleasures

[1] सर्वभूतस्थमात्मानं सर्वभूतानि चात्मनि ।
ईक्षते योगयुक्तात्मा सर्वत्र समदर्शनः ॥

Bhagavadgītā, VI, 29.

[2] यो मां पश्यति सर्वत्र सर्वं च मयि पश्यति ।
तस्याहं न प्रणश्यामि स च मे न प्रणश्यति ॥

Ibid., VI, 30.

and pains as his own is esteemed, O Arjuna, as a perfect Yogin."[1] "Whatever action a man would not like if done to himself by another, that he shall refrain from doing to others."[2] Among the acts of charity enjoined by Manu is Pūrta which consists in the construction of works of utility to the people, such as wells and tanks, gardens, etc. This is only an illustrative list of the works of public utility which are recommended by way of charity.

Various other charges have been brought against Hinduism by Mr. John McKenzie which are mostly the result of misconception and prejudice. For example, he considers even some of the admitted virtues of the Hindus to be of savage origin and due to other motives than a sense of duty or altruism.[3] His description of Hindu ethics as anti-social[4] is a terminological inexactitude, for what he means is probably that it is non-social. These charges have been effectively refuted by Prof. Washburn Hopkins in his *Ethics of India* and it is unnecessary to deal with them here.

[1] आत्मौपम्येन सर्वत्र समं पश्यति योऽर्जुन ।
सुखं वा यदि वा दुःखं स योगी परमो मतः ॥

Bhagavadgītā, VI, 32.

[2] यदन्यैर्विहितं नेच्छेदात्मनः कर्म पूरुषः ।
न तत्परेषु कुर्वीत जानन्नप्रियमात्मनः ॥

Mahābhārata, Śāntiparva, 260, 20.

[3] *See* J. McKenzie: *Hindu Ethics*, p. 97.

[4] *Ibid.*, pp. 144, 213.

As regards the criticism of Max Müller that the ethics of the Vedānta philosophy lacks inspiration to strengthen the manly qualities required for the practical side of life, it may be pointed out that it inculcates the virtues of courage, fearlessness of death, fortitude and single-minded devotion to duty. There can be no stronger or more closely reasoned or eloquent call to duty than that contained in the second chapter of the *Gītā*. The followers of proselytising and militant religions are ordinarily disposed to claim a monopoly of truth in favour of their religions, and are not inclined to do justice to the merits of other religions. They forget the history of early Christianity and seek an appraisement of the ethics of other systems in the light of the life and thought of the nineteenth or twentieth century. They are tempted to look at the motes in other people's eyes, overlooking the beams in their own. They are inclined to ascribe to the influence of Christian ethics movements due to the forces of scientific discovery, rationalism and the expansion of the range of human interests and sympathies brought about by modern improvements in the means of communication. None of the ethical systems, especially those founded on scriptural authority and tradition, can claim to be perfect. Every system has got its own crudities, defects and illogicalities.[1] It would be unfair to institute a comparison between the ethical

[1] The doctrines of original sin, predestination and damnation of unbaptised infants are a few of the instances of Christian doctrines which appear strange and unintelligible to the Hindu mind.

notions which find a place in the ancient literature of any nation with those prevalent at the present time and under modern conditions. Many of the defects of Hindu ethics which have been noticed in the previous chapters have their parallel in other systems of ethics also. If we find a spirit of discrimination between class and class or between the sexes in the system of law and justice recorded in the old Hindu law-books, we find the same spirit permeating European jurisprudence down to very recent times and still characterising the laws relating to the treatment of the coloured races by the Whites. The inferiority of women in legal status and rights was as much a feature of the law in Christian Europe as it was of the Hindu law. The immunities and privileges enjoyed by the Brahmins in regard to taxation and other matters had their counterpart in the various immunities and privileges enjoyed by the nobles and the clergy down to the end of the eighteenth century. If we find a lack of sense of proportion in the importance attached to transgressions of ethical rules and of ceremonial, ritual, or merely conventional rules in the Hindu law-books, we find the same tendency in Christian ethical systems also. Questions of orthodoxy and fasting appeared to the popular mind immeasurably more important than the fundamental principles of right and wrong. It is stated by Lecky that "a law of Charlemagne, and also a law of the Saxons, condemned to death any man who ate meat in Lent, unless the priest was satisfied that it was a matter of absolute necessity."[1] The rules and restrictions regarding the observance of the Sabbath in Christian countries were quite as absurd as those to be found in the Hindu ceremonial law. It is stated by one writer that the Puritans hanged their cats on Monday for catching mice on Sunday. A law in Connecticut forbade a man to kiss his wife on Sunday.[2] In England in the seventeenth century persons were punished for hanging out clothes to dry on Sunday and for walking about. Scotch clergymen taught their congregations that it was sinful on a Sunday to save a vessel in distress and that religion required that the ship and crew should be left to perish.[3] Some of the Hindu law-books forbade a man to eat in the company of his wife.[4]

The fact that parallels can be found in other countries for the defects or absurdities in the Hindu system of ethics would not justify any attempt to cling to antiquated notions and practices. The Christian nations of Europe have been gradually discarding their superstitions and taboos and their belief in miracles, myths and legends and re-examining and re-shaping their beliefs and institutions in the light of reason and modern scientific knowledge. In this country we have not gone sufficiently far on the same route owing to the comparatively more recent advent of scienti-

[1] W. E. H. Lecky: *History of European Morals (Library edition)*, Vol. II, p. 257.

[2] P. Smith: *A History of Modern Culture*, Vol. I, p. 499.

[3] E. Westermarck: *The Origin and Development of the Moral Ideas*, Vol. II, p. 289.

[4] *E.g., Bodhāyana*, I, i, 2, 3; *Yājñavalkya*, I, 131.

fic knowledge and the lack of general education among the people. Even as it is, many an inroad has been made into the domain of orthodoxy and the strict regulations of the ceremonial law have been losing their hold upon the minds of people. No living organism can escape the necessity for adaptation to changes of environment, and Hindu society is no exception to the rule. But there is still a large mass of beliefs and conventional practices surviving in Hindu society which cannot stand the challenge of reason. The fact that there are numerous restrictions in the Hindu Dharma Śāstra which have deservedly fallen into disuse tells against the claim of eternal validity ascribed to them by the orthodox believers in Sanātana Dharma. If the injunctions of the Dharma Śāstra cannot be accepted in their entirety as of a binding character and suitable to the present age, the only test by which we can determine whether and how far the old rules should be still regarded as binding under present conditions is the application of the principles of rationalism and utilitarianism. Let me give a few instances of restrictions contained in the Dharma Śāstras which are rapidly falling into disuse. The prohibition of the learning of foreign languages, of foreign travel and of various occupations is no longer observed. Marriages of a brother's children with the sister's children are allowed in many parts of southern India. But the marriage between members of the same Gotra is still tabooed and regarded as illegal. The rules regarding impurity from birth or death which prescribe more or less long periods of pollution of the relations are still in force, though not observed with the same rigour. The marriage of a younger sister or brother before the elder which was condemned as sinful and entailed a penance is not regarded with the same feeling of disapproval as it used to excite.

Apart from those defects which the Hindu system of ethics shares with other systems, the main charges to which it is open are the overwhelming predominance of ritualism, the repression of freedom of action and individual initiative and the development to extraordinary lengths of the system of caste with its fissiparous tendencies. Every system of ethics which has been moulded by sacerdotal influences tends to lay stress on ceremonies and loses sight of the distinction between fundamentals and trivialities. But religious ceremonies occupy such a large place in the daily life of the twice-born classes and especially of the Brahmins that they do not leave sufficient time for attention to secular matters and they colour the whole outlook of the orthodox Brahmin upon life and distort his sense of the values of ceremonial and other matters. Partly for this reason and partly because of the traditional authority of the scriptures and the meticulous regulation of the daily life of the Brahmin down to the smallest details, there has been a tendency towards the repression of freedom in external life.

The hold of ritualism at the present moment is partly due to the survival of a superstitious belief in its magical efficacy and partly to a desire for social conformity. One obvious method of reducing the excessive attachment to ritualism would be the translation into the vernaculars of all the sacred texts which are used in connection with the rituals. The fact that the texts are all written in Sanskrit which is not understood by the masses and is seldom understood even by the officiating priest at these rituals and the sonorousness of the Sanskrit language lend a peculiar glamour of distinction, solemnity and mystery to the rituals, which many of them would fail to command on their own merits. Ignorance of the meaning of the words employed heightens the feeling of mystery, just as the intonation of the prayers in the Latin tongue deepens the feeling of solemnity in the minds of the worshippers in the Catholic churches. The sacred texts used in connection with rituals should be translated in a dignified but simple style so as to be understood of the people. The orthodox may think that the sacramental efficacy of the Mantras may be lost by translation into the vulgar tongue. Those who wish to use the ancient language of the rituals need not be constrained to adopt the vernacular version. But the existence of the vernacular version will help towards a just appreciation of the significance of the rituals and prayers. The vernacularisation of our ritualistic literature will have the same effect upon religious thought as the translation of the Bible in Protestant countries.

It has sometimes been remarked by foreign writers on Hindu ethics that the virtues inculcated in the Hindu sacred books are more or less of a commonplace character and that the maxims seldom rise above popular morality. This remark does not do justice to the ethical ideals evolved by the Hindu sages, which have not merely found expression in their sacred literature, but have also influenced the life and thought of the people of the country. The virtues of universal kindliness and benevolence, of suffering and self-sacrifice for the sake of principle or from altruistic motives, of forgiveness and courage, of devotion and humility of spirit are as highly cherished and admired by Hindus as by the followers of any other religion. A comparative study of the ethical notions embodied in the leading religious systems of the world discloses the absence of any fundamental differences on the essentials of morality. There may be differences of emphasis on particular virtues or rules of conduct. But on the whole, there is a substantial similarity of views in regard to the rules of conduct which should be followed. It is not suggested that there are no differences whatever between one religion and another regarding the relative values of particular virtues or that there is no difference in the contribution made by different religions towards the development of ethical ideals. For instance, the claim may with justice be made on behalf of Hinduism that it has made a valuable contribution to the ethical culture of the world in several important directions.

I may now proceed to refer to some of the principles peculiar to Hinduism or upon which special emphasis has been laid by it far more than by any of the other religious systems.

(1) The doctrine of Karma teaches that everyone must win his salvation by his own work, character and effort, that he cannot hope to rise on the backs of others or by the charity or the sufferings of others and that he is bound to reap what he has sown and cannot hope to escape the consequences of his own acts. This doctrine is a much stronger incentive to the spirit of manly self-reliance and self-improvement than the doctrine of vicarious atonement or redemption.

(2) Hinduism dwells persistently upon the importance of self-discipline and self-control for the regulation and co-ordination of human impulses and instincts for the perfection of character.

(3) In no occidental religion has the doctrine of Ahiṁsā or non-injury been proclaimed as one of universal scope or assigned such an important place in the ethical scheme. It would be easy to point out, as the virtuous butcher (Dharma-vyādha) does in the *Mahābhārata,* that the maxim is not always or strictly practicable. But it cannot detract from the merit of conduct conforming to this principle or from the value of the ideal as a humanising influence in the formation of character.

(4) The positive duty of kindness to the lower animals is nowhere insisted upon to the same extent as in Hinduism. The duty is based upon

a recognition of the sanctity of all life and especially animal life and a belief in the sensitiveness of animals to suffering. It is absurd to suggest, as has been done by some writers on comparative ethics, that this duty of kindness to the lower animals is connected with the doctrine of transmigration of souls or with what has been described as zoolatry.

(5) Hinduism has always been characterised by a spirit of toleration towards other religions and has hardly ever indulged in the persecution of the followers of other religions. It has never put forward the arrogant claim to a monopoly of truth and never denied the possibility of the followers of other creeds obtaining salvation according to the ways of their own religion. It does not condemn the followers of other creeds to eternal damnation. The ultimate goal of all religions is believed to be the same, though the ways of reaching it may be different. It has been suggested by some writers that tolerance of other creeds is a characteristic of polytheism. Pure Hinduism is essentially monotheistic. But the Hindu does not believe that his mind is capable of grasping the Deity in its essence or in the totality of its manifestations and he is humble enough to feel that it is not possible for the human mind to perceive anything more than an infinitesimal aspect of the truth and that different minds may possibly perceive different aspects of the Infinite Being. A feeling of certainty about things perceived by the senses is justifiable. Confidence about things which have not been perceived, but may

be verified, may be also justifiable. But dogmatism about things which can be neither perceived nor verified nor felt to be logically inevitable is inexcusable. The claim that any one religion is the sole vehicle or embodiment of truth and that all other religions are false is the height of presumption.

(6) It is the glory of Hinduism that it has never interfered with or discouraged freedom of thought, speculation or opinion, has never persecuted people for heresy and has never placed a ban upon freedom of discussion.[1] Hinduism was specially concerned with the preservation of the social structure and it enforced conformity in matters of external conduct, but not in matters of opinion or doctrine.

(7) In dealing with the mutual relations of members of society Hinduism has generally been disposed to lay stress upon obligations rather than rights. From the standpoint of individualism which was in the ascendant in England in the nineteenth century this might be regarded as a defect. But from the standpoint of collectivism which has come to the fore in the present century, this insistence upon duties instead of rights must be regarded as a praiseworthy feature of Hinduism.

(8) At a time when ethical speculation is perplexed about the derivation of the sense of moral obligation and the question whether it should be

[1] *See* Rhys Davids: *Lectures on Indian Buddhism*, pp. 4, 229-231. This is in striking contrast with the intolerance of Christianity towards freedom of thought. *See also* J. B. Bury: *A History of Freedom of Thought.*

traced to external sanctions or to the dictates of the moral sense or moral self, the metaphysical doctrine of the identity of the Atman or individual self with the Brahman or universal soul affords a valuable hypothesis of the origin of the notion of obligation and is perhaps more satisfactory than the intutional theory.

(9) In connection with the question of the ends of human action, the doctrine of Puruṣārthas recognises a plurality of duly co-ordinated ends and is far more in accordance with the realities of life than the analytical and rather barren quest for a single *summum bonum* under which all the other ends of human action can be subsumed.

(10) The doctrine of Adhikāribheda or relativity with reference to capacity, qualifications and conditions is throughout recognised and implied in Hindu ethics as regards the moral ends and as regards the rules of conduct. Ends and rules have alike to be adapted to the capacities of individuals, to their status in society, to their conditions and occupations. The Hindu code of ethics is not a Procrustean bed to which all individuals should be adapted irrespective of varying qualifications and conditions. While there are universal rules of conduct applicable to all persons and under all conditions, the Hindu code recognises the existence and necessity of special codes as well as the need for the flexibility of injunctions. It is unfortunate that in the hands of the latter-day law-givers the principle of flexibility and adaptation has not been sufficiently borne in mind and that too often

Nibandhanakāras or digest-writers have endeavoured to petrify the rules of conduct.

The ethical conceptions which have been embodied in Hindu literature and have moulded the life and thought of Hindus for ages have now been brought into contact with those of the rest of the civilised world and are undergoing transformation under the impact of new economic conditions, scientific knowledge, western civilisation and literature and the social and political movements and ideas of Europe.

CHAPTER XII

MORAL PROGRESS

In the course of these lectures I have pointed out that Hindu ethics has undergone changes, though very slowly and gradually, from time to time in response to the varying conditions of the times. I have pleaded for a re-examination of our ethical system. The old rules have to be re-interpreted and modified where necessary. The process of change which has been set on foot is sure to be accelerated by the influence of the various factors to which I have referred. It has been truly said that "progress is sure and continuous in proportion as it depends upon the principle of tradition, *i.e.*, in proportion as the gains of the past can be handed on and form a capital for advancing the operations of the future."[1]

We may perhaps pause here to inquire whether the changes which have already taken place in the ethical conceptions of our society are changes for the better. The question of ethical progress has often been discussed by writers on ethics and sociology. It would probably be conceded that, as compared with the primitive and backward races, the civilised races of the world have attained to a much higher level of conception of their duties to their

[1] L. T. Hobhouse: *Morals in Evolution*, Vol. II, p. 281.

fellow-beings in society. But it is held by several thinkers that after a certain stage of civilisation has been reached, there has been no appreciable progress towards improvement in conduct as distinguished from progress in ethical conceptions and theory. It is also true that "moral progress (to assume provisionally that it is a reality) does not proceed continuously in a straight line. It does not affect all branches of the moral law simultaneously, nor does it advance step by step with the growth of civilisation."[1] Civilisation in this connection may be held to denote a greater command over the powers of nature, a growing enlargement of the domain of knowledge and an increase in the conveniences, luxuries and amenities of life and in the facilities for education, travel and social intercourse. It has been pointed out by Lecky that high intellectual and material civilisation has often co-existed with moral depravity and that the conditions of intellectual growth are in some respects unfavourable to moral growth. He remarks that civilisation is very favourable to the gentler and social virtues, and where slavery does not exist, to the industrial virtues. But it is in general not equally favourable to the production of self-sacrifice, enthusiasm, reverence or chastity.[2] This remark would require a large qualification in view of our experience during the Great War and since. While the virtues of reverence and chastity are visibly on the wane,

[1] L. T. Hobhouse: *Morals in Evolution*, Vol. I, p. 35.
[2] W. E. H. Lecky: *History of European Morals* (*Library edition*), Vol. I, p. 157.

an imminent sense of national peril has been found to be capable of evoking heights of self-sacrifice and enthusiasm not inferior to those attained in any previous period of history. The cult of Bolshevism has, in spite of many repellent features, evoked a wonderful spirit of self-sacrifice and enthusiasm from its adherents. There have been writers who have held that the doctrine of evolution holds good in the sphere of social relations as much as in the sphere of external nature and that evolution implies progress. On the other hand, it has been contended with great force that evolution is a neutral term compatible with a change either for the better or for the worse. That societies have undergone decay as well as improvement is matter of common knowledge. I do not consider it necessary to refer to the larger issues raised by historians of progress whether the movement of humanity can be described as a movement of universal progress towards a desirable goal of existence, or whether such progress is sure and continuous. The question with which we are immediately concerned is whether in respect of moral standards, rules or character and conduct, humanity has been moving towards the conception and realisation of a higher standard. The ancient Hindus believed in the theory of cycles of growth, decay and dissolution and in the repetition of history in the universe. Like European thinkers of ancient and mediæval times, our ancestors also placed the golden age of the world in a legendary past and believed in the ethical degeneration of the human race, but with this difference, that the Hindu theory of the cycles of the Yugas permits us to believe in recurring cycles of Yugas and in the recurrence of the golden age at a future time also. Leaving aside the question of moral conduct for the present, it may be fairly contended that there has been on the whole a rise to a higher conception of ethical duties. It seems to me that the ideal which moral rules should keep in view and by which they should be judged is the ideal of universalistic hedonism or utilitarianism. The ideal of a perfect character may be explained and interpreted as one which is conducive to this ideal of universal happiness or utilitarianism. Judging by this standard, we may accept the conclusion of Prof. Hobhouse that there has been a progress in ethical conceptions as a result of the application of rationalism and humanitarianism.[1] By way of illustration we may refer to the doctrine of equality of rights and opportunities for all human beings, the appreciation of civil and political liberty[2] so far as compatible with the equal liberty of others, the appreciation of the need for harmonious development of our faculties, the disapproval of class and caste distinctions and privileges, the recognition of the claim of women to equality of treatment, the abolition of slavery and serfdom, the advance from parochialism to national or international ideals, the treatment of prisoners of war, the conception of duty for duty's

[1] *See* L. T. Hobhouse: *Morals in Evolution*, Vol. II, p. 264 ff.

[2] The prevalence of dictatorship in Italy, Germany, Russia and other countries is, I am inclined to believe, an abnormal and temporary phase due to the present economic and political conditions.

sake, the disbelief in hell as an ethical sanction, the refined conceptions of the Deity, the growth of humanitarianism and the extension of our sympathies to peoples of other countries. In so far as character is dependent upon inherited impulses and instincts, the doctrine that acquired characteristics are not inherited weakens the belief in an improvement of our innate character. The laws of heredity are still obscure and few thinkers venture to affirm that there has been a real improvement in the innate moral character of human beings. Buckle thought that in what might be called the innate and original morals of mankind there had been no progress, and Huxley expressed a much more gloomy view of human character. Rousseau dwelt upon the virtues of the noble savage and was of opinion that morals fall and rise in correspondence with the progress and decline of the arts and that civilisation produces a degeneracy of character. Gibbon allows us to "acquiesce in the pleasing conclusion that every age of the world has increased and still increases the happiness, the knowledge and perhaps the virtue of the human race." A more cautious conclusion has been adopted by writers in this century, more especially as the result of the disillusionment produced by the Great War and its aftermath. Hobhouse expressed the opinion that the question whether, morally considered, the human breed has in fact improved is by no means easy to settle empirically. He was disinclined to give an affirmative answer to the question whether the actual improvement in our conduct as compared with that of our ancestors is greater than we might expect, or even as much as we might expect.[1] Bury was of opinion that against the technical progress made by mankind must be set down the exploitation and sufferings of industrial workers and that the distress of intense economic competition, the heavier preparation for modern war and the very increase of material ease seemed unavoidably to involve conditions inconsistent with universal happiness and that the communications which linked the peoples of the world together modified the methods of warfare instead of bringing peace. The triumphs of philanthropy did not seem to him to affect the general conclusion that, while knowledge is indefinitely progressive, there is no good reason for sanguine hope that man is perfectible or that universal happiness is attainable.[2]

Yet in spite of the pessimism entertained by so many writers regarding the moral improvement of human nature, we cannot treat ethical speculation as of no value or view with indifference the problem of the basis of moral rules. As our knowledge increases and the spirit of rationalism grows, it is impossible for us to rest content with the traditional foundations of morality and we cannot help seeking to discover a rational basis for the empirical rules which have been followed by society. Nor is it possible for us to ignore the necessity for changes in our rules of conduct and social institutions in response to the growing complexity of

[1] L. T. Hobhouse: *Morals in Evolution,* Vol. II, p. 283.
[2] J. B. Bury: *The Idea of Progress,* pp. 332-333.

our daily altering environment. As the spirit of inquiry grows, the system of authoritarian morality must necessarily be displaced by a system of reflective and rational morality. We may be liable to make mistakes and our reason may furnish only a dim light for guidance and be unable to foresee all the consequences of a change. But we cannot acquiesce in the position that the last word of wisdom is to be found in the systems of the ancient writers or in revelation. The ideas of relativity and development must necessarily furnish the foundation of any modern ethical system intended to secure harmony between man and his environment.

In connection with the question of the extent to which human conduct has actually conformed to the moral standards of the time, it would be difficult to assert of any country that a comparison of its moral attainment in one age with another exhibits moral progress in all human relations, or in other words, a progress all along the line. There may be a decline in some virtues and an increase in others. For instance, there may be a decline in the practice of hospitality and an increase in the manifestation of sympathy for distant people in distress. Any conclusion as to the progress of morals from one epoch to another can at best amount only to a rough generalisation subject to qualifications and exceptions.

It is also a difficult question if we seek to compare the degree of happiness enjoyed by the people of any country in one age with that attained by them in anbther. In so far as the feeling of happiness is subjective, it is not easy to make an estimate for purposes of comparison. The tendency of people to adjust themselves to their external conditions is a factor which promotes a feeling of reconcilement to their surroundings. On the other hand the very process of adjustment introduces new factors in the environment and gives rise to fresh problems. It is also a characteristic of human nature that it never feels perfectly contented, but is always discovering new wants and fresh grounds of dissatisfaction. Making allowance, however, for these considerations, it is possible to form an opinion as to the extent to which the external conditions of happiness are available and how far they are distributed among different sections of the people. It is thus not impossible to form a rough estimate as to the manner in which the social institutions and moral rules obtaining in any country have contributed to its happiness and welfare.

I have observed that the disbelief in the tortures of hell as a sanction of morality indicates progress in our ethical conceptions. Right conduct proceeding from a virtuous disposition and without the expectation of reward or the fear of punishment is undoubtedly more meritorious than conduct prompted by these motives. This judgment will hold good whether the conceptions of heaven and hell were based upon fact or imagination. Whether the growing disbelief in such external sanctions has been favourable to the maintenance of morality is a question upon which it is not easy to express an opinion with confidence irrespective of the degree of intellectual education of the society concerned. Christianity, Islam and popular Hinduism have all relied upon these future sanctions as aids to morality. Assuming that there is no foundation in fact for the conceptions of heaven and hell, it is one of those cases in which, as Lecky says, we owe more to our illusions than to our knowledge, and superstitions often become essential elements of happiness. Whether in the interests of speculative truth we should carry on a campaign to shatter these religious beliefs is a question which wise people may hesitate to answer in the affirmative. The *Gītā* warns the wise against the danger of unsettling the minds of the ignorant who cling to the traditional codes of conduct.[1] It would perhaps be best to leave these beliefs alone and trust to the general influence of education. The modernist Christian and Vedantin have alike abandoned the belief in hell, though on different grounds. Apart from the withdrawal of the support given to morality by the fear of future punishments, a further danger from the orthodox point of view consists in the probable disappearance of heaven also. One may reasonably entertain a doubt whether the disbelief in these sanctions can be pronounced to be an unmixed good in all stages of society.

Yet another question of great importance in connection with the subject of moral progress is

[1] *Bhagavadgītā*, III, 26.

whether dispositions which would be regarded as virtues or vices in one country or at one time are necessarily to be so regarded in other countries or at other times. Let us take, for instance, the trait of mind indicated by the word 'individualism' or 'patriotism'. The joint family system which has prevailed in Hindu society has tended to check the growth of individualism and has fostered the habit of mutual help within the family circle. But the institution has to a considerable extent retarded the growth of a spirit of self-reliance, individual initiative and enterprise. Coupled with the doctrine of self-acquisition it may be contended that the institution furnishes opportunities for the cultivation of individualism as well as altruism. It is not possible to discuss here all the advantages of the system; but it is sufficient to remark that the system has proved to be unsuitable to modern conditions and is fast breaking up. The growth of individualism has in England and in America reached a height which may be considered undesirable and might be regarded by the socialist and the communist as incompatible with the welfare of society. While the cultivation of individualism is likely to be beneficial in India, it may not be equally so in the case of countries where it has been already developed to a maximum. Similarly while nationalism and patriotism are virtues to be encouraged and developed in India, the spirit of nationalism has reached undesirable lengths in Europe and America. Nationalism and patriotism have till recently been universally recognised as fundamental civic virtues enabling societies to preserve and defend themselves against attacks, to maintain their self-respect and to preserve and develop the special gifts, traits and culture which have enabled every nation or country to make some useful contribution to the welfare and progress of humanity. Down to the time of the Great War no one would have considered it necessary to attempt a vindication of these virtues. The aggressive nationalism which brought on the Great War and still survives, which has led to the conquest and exploitation of backward territories and races, and the economic imperialism and competition which menace international peace have led some thinkers in England and India to denounce nationalism as an anti-world sentiment and the desire for economic self-sufficiency as not merely a fallacy, but as a vice and a peril. But the peoples in several of the backward countries, though fulfilling several of the conditions necessary to constitute a nation, are still so deficient in the spirit of combination and co-operation and in the essential art of self-defence that it is necessary for them to acquire the virtues which make a united nation. It is only when they have sufficiently developed an effective sense of nationality that they will be fit for admission to a federation of states or the parliament of the world. Every European or American nation is fond of preaching to other nations the advantages of cultivating an international mind and throwing their doors open to an influx of foreign goods from countries which have long since attained industrial development and predominance. Other instances can be easily given where qualities of mind and character which require to be cultivated in one country require to be discouraged in others. We are thus brought back again to the necessity of giving due recognition to the principle of relativity in the formulation of moral rules and ends.

The fact that certain virtues have declined and that other virtues have grown in popular estimation does not necessarily enable us to pronounce an opinion for or against the moral progress of society on the whole. It may be that the new distribution of moral values is better suited to the conditions of the time and possibly better calculated to advance the well-being and happiness of mankind. It must be remembered that moral codes have come into existence for the benefit of human beings and not human beings for the benefit of moral codes. The most fundamental rules of conduct which prevail in nearly all civilised societies have acquired their importance from the fact that the experience of humanity for ages past has shown them to be essential for our well-being as members of society. It is, however, conceivable that radical and far-reaching changes in our conditions of existence, social surroundings and intellectual climate may produce changes in our moral values or in the distribution of emphasis among them. Even a writer of the intuitionist school like Lecky, who was inclined to believe in the immutable character of moral rules, was obliged to admit that, while the essential nature of virtue and vice is unaltered, there is a perpetual and, in some branches, an orderly and necessary change as society advances both in the proportionate value attached to different virtues in theory and in the perfection in which they are realised in practice. He remarks that there are virtues which are continually dying away with advancing civilisation and that while there may be in societies such a thing as moral improvement, there is rarely or never, on a large scale, such a thing as unmixed improvement.[1]

[1] W. E. H. Lecky: *History of European Morals* (*Library edition*), Vol. I, p. 154.

CHAPTER XIII

THE DRIFT OF MODERN TENDENCIES AND THE FUTURE

SINCE the advent of the British in India and especially after the introduction of English education, India has been brought under the influence of Western civilisation and culture. The clash of the Eastern and Western systems of civilisation and culture has produced far-reaching changes in our ideas and outlook upon life. The vast improvements in communications, the increase in the habit of travelling and in international trade and the enormous and unprecedented growth of facilities for diffusion of news and knowledge have linked the countries of the world together and increased their mutual dependence on a scale hitherto unknown. The Great War furnished a palpable demonstration of the inter-dependence of the countries of the world for weal or woe; and the economic depression through which the whole world is passing has driven this fact into the minds of all people. As an important unit of the British Empire, India could not help being drawn into the vortex of world forces. The dissemination of ideas knows no barriers of race, country or distance. It would be a marvel if India remained unaffected by the vast changes which have taken place in the economic, sociological and moral ideas of the world. Our religious and ethical conceptions, our social and political ideas, our civic, national and economic ideals are all undergoing rapid change under the stress of the new world conditions. They have been assailed by the changes in the economic life of the country, by scientific progress and the spread of rationalism and by intercourse with the other countries of the world. It would be impossible, even if desirable, for any country to keep aloof from the rest of the world, or to prevent the social adjustments which are a necessary consequence of the new factors in our environment.

Let me briefly refer to the changes which are rapidly taking place in ideas and institutions in the civilised world and proceed to inquire whether we shall be able to escape similar changes. It was remarked by Bertrand Russell that 150 years of science had proved more explosive than 5,000 years of pre-scientific culture and that science has become an important factor in determining the everyday life of everyday people. A Rousseau or a Gandhi may preach the blessings of plain-living and high-thinking or may sigh for the Arcadian simplicity of life led by our old ancestors. They may deal in vague generalities without indicating how many and which of the conveniences of life and other advantages procured by scientific inventions we should forego, and without proving that plain-living is necessarily accompanied by high-thinking. But the common sense even of the country-side which has learnt the use of the railway and the motor bus in the place of the bullock cart will protest against any return to the old days. As pointed out by Bertrand Russell, a return to nature, if it were taken seriously, would involve the death by starvation of some ninety per cent. of the population of civilised countries.[1] Even more than the part played by scientific knowledge in increasing the command of man over nature and supplying his material wants is the part played by it in imparting a new outlook upon life and encouraging the habit of using our reason and limiting the province of faith. Every belief and institution has to submit to the challenge of reason and justify itself. Even religion has been obliged to make terms with the spirit of science and come to an understanding as to the respective provinces of reason and faith. Fortunately for this reconciliation, science and religion are now alike inspired by a spirit of humility and decreasing dogmatism. The religion of the modernist Christian is far removed from that of the primitive or the mediæval church. The modernist Christian does not believe in the cosmogony of the Old Testament or in the special creation of man or in miracles or in the punishments of hell. The modernist does not look upon Christianity as a system of ethics or code of rules for conduct, but only as 'an outlook and a manner of thinking and acting and a standard of values'. The personality of Christ is held to be a fountain of righteousness and spiritual life. In many quarters there is a tendency to reduce the conception of the Deity to a combination of abstract qualities or

[1] *The Scientific Outlook*, p. 145.

values. As regards the actual condition of religious belief in western countries, the description given by eminent writers shows that among the educated classes religious faith has been steadily losing ground. Dean Inge remarks that many of the English churches would be much emptier if the Gospel were taught in them,[1] and Bishop Gore says that "to-day at least as conspicuously as orthodox theology, the accepted moral standard of Christian tradition is being assailed with contempt, with ridicule and with indignant argument—not only the morality of sex, but also the whole idea of self-denial and the service of the weak by the strong. The current popular literature is demanding above all things free individual self-expression, unshackled by parental or ecclesiastical authority or by considerations of humility or chastity."[2] The opinion that there has been a great decay of religious beliefs in England is amply supported by the facts brought together by Mr. Joad in his *Present and Future of Religion* in the chapter on the 'Drift from Churches'. If this is the state of religious belief in the Christian world, what is the position in India? It is difficult to make any general statement applicable to all classes of the people. We may divide the people into different classes according to the character and intensity of their beliefs. There is probably more religious belief among the masses and especially among women, mixed up with a very large amount of superstition. Among the literate

[1] *Christian Ethics and Modern Problems*, p. 398.
[2] *Philosophy of the Good Life*, p. 14.

and educated classes we may distinguish various shades of thought. Leaving out the class of people who do not care to think about religion and are indifferent to it, but appreciate the convenience of conformity to established conventions, there are, as in other countries, the sceptics and the believers. Among the believers again there are those who may be called revivalists who cling to all the old tenets and practices, discovering fanciful explanations under the guise of allegory, symbolism or esoteric truth. There are others who entertain a belief in the essential tenets of Hinduism and endeavour to reconcile their religious beliefs with the requirements of reason as best they can. While it would be difficult to hazard any statement with reference to the numbers and proportions of the persons belonging to these classes, it would probably be true to hold that the proportion of religiously minded people in this country is much larger than in other countries and certainly not less.

So far as I can see, there is no likelihood of any mass movement towards conversion to any other religion, except perhaps in the case of the depressed classes who may be tempted to embrace one or other of the proselytising religions, if the evil of untouchability is not soon eradicated. So far as the intelligentsia of the country are concerned, they believe that no religion can claim any intrinsic superiority over the others, that Hinduism is as capable of adaptation as other religions and that the guidance which the purer forms of Hinduism can furnish in matters of religion or ethics is quite as valuable as that to be found in other systems. This is the reason why neither Christianity nor Islam has been able to make any progress among the intelligentsia of the Hindu population. Hinduism has a far greater power of accommodation (far too much in the opinion of many) than the other creeds of the world and would have less difficulty in reconciling its philosophical basis with the conclusions of modern scientific thought. I do not wish to suggest that in matters of culture any nation should adopt self-sufficiency or exclusiveness as its motto. But there is *prima facie* a presumption in favour of long-established creeds as better suited to the instincts, cravings, temperaments and inherited culture of the people among whom they have obtained. If the pretensions of creeds to mutual superiority and attempts at proselytism are abandoned, there will be a greater disposition and tendency to an interchange of ideas to the advantage of humanity.

One great handicap under which Hinduism labours is its load of ritualism and ceremonial observances. The sooner its followers can lighten the load and devote themselves to the essentials of religion, the greater will be its chances of survival. The social institution of caste which has been developed in India to such fantastic lengths is also bound to disappear. But its disappearance need not affect Hinduism as a religion; it will, on the other hand, help the promotion of unity in India. The orthodox who believe in the letter of the law may wonder at these reflections and some of them may even think that if caste and ceremonialism are eliminated, there will be nothing left that is distinctive of Hinduism. We need not be sorry if the great religions of the world reduce their points of difference and develop their points of agreement. But I think that this view does injustice to the fundamentals of the Hindu religion and its contribution to the religious thought of humanity. Other critics may ask whether an institution like caste which has grown up for ages and has withstood the onslaughts of alien civilisations is likely to perish. The new forces to which Hinduism is now exposed are altogether of a different character. The spirit of rationalism and the influence of the scientific outlook, as Bertrand Russell calls it, are far more powerful and penetrating than foreign armies and governments and are bound to give a death-blow to institutions which cannot furnish satisfactory reasons for their continuance. Signs have not been wanting of the beginning of the process of disintegration of the system of caste. The three distinctive features of caste have been restrictions on occupations, inter-dining, and inter-marriage. The first set of restrictions has totally disappeared. The second has begun to disappear in the towns, and the third also is beginning to give way, though only slowly and in a very small number of cases. Inter-marriages between sub-sections of the main castes are daily increasing. Mixed marriages between members of the different main castes, not merely of men of higher caste with women of lower caste, but of women of higher caste with men of lower caste, are creeping in. There have also been cases of the marriage of Hindus with Europeans and Americans and other races like the Burmese and the Siamese. The question may be raised whether inter-marriages between the main castes or mixed marriages between the different races are desirable from the point of view of eugenics or of the happiness of the persons contracting such marriages. How far marriages of this sort would be conducive to the happiness of the parties to the marriages is a question which will have to be decided by the parties themselves. We can only note that differences in habits, ways of living and manners are, more often than not, likely to cause friction in the intimate intercourse of daily life in the home. From the point of view of eugenics, if there is no racial disparity, there is no reason for the apprehension of disastrous consequences merely on the ground of racial difference. Unfortunately the system of marriage that obtains among us does not pay sufficient regard to eugenic considerations such as are recommended by the ancient Hindu law-givers or by modern biologists. More importance is attached to astrological and mercenary considerations than to purely eugenic considerations. Impatient social reformers and foreign critics who cast reproaches at the very slow progress of inter-marriages between the main castes do not realise how deeply the institution of marriage enters into the structure of society and morals and how a hasty and violent loosening of the bonds which have held the social fabric may produce a moral chaos. How deep-rooted the prejudices against race and colour are can be seen from the acceptance by the German nation of the new laws propounded by Hitler for the preservation of the purity of the German race and the prohibition of marriages and sex relations between Germans and other races.

Turning back to the condition of religious belief, I am inclined to think that the same forces which have operated in other countries to produce a decline of religious faith are also at work in India and that we cannot expect to escape the corrosive influences of modern thought. Beliefs in miracles and legends and in dogmas that are incapable of proof will tend to decline. The sense of the immense mystery surrounding our existence, the religious instinct and the craving for its satisfaction will, however, remain. Religion for the developed modern consciousness is described by Mr. Joad as "a vague and uncertain intimation of value in the universe, an intimation that is accompanied by an emotion of reverence and awed worship."[1] The purer forms of the Hindu religion may expect to have at least as good a chance of survival as any other of the great religions of the world.

Other departments of life and thought in the modern world have also been profoundly affected by the new economic conditions and other factors which have been adverted to above. The two institutions upon which the whole structure of

[1] C. E. M. Joad: *The Present and Future of Religion*, p. 198.

civilised society has been based are family and property. They are inextricably bound up with each other and any weakening of the foundations of either is bound to react on the vitality of the other. This century has witnessed in western countries startling changes in the long-established notions of the relations between the sexes and a growing disregard for the old codes of marriage and sexual ethics. The change has amounted to a complete upheaval in Russia and though the other countries of Europe and America have not been convulsed in the same manner, it cannot be said that they have escaped the influence of the shock. It is the rising generation of youth that has been specially affected by the influence of the new movement for freedom of self-expression. The world was startled a few years ago by the publication of Judge Ben Lindsey's books on the *Revolt of Modern Youth* and the *Companionate Marriage* which drew attention to the great changes in morals which had been taking place among the rising generation in American social life. Volumes have been written upon the disorganisation of family life, the decreasing sanctity of marriage, the increase in the number of divorces and the tendency to the formation of extra-marital and temporary intimacies. For some time it was said that the picture drawn by Ben Lindsey was highly coloured and did not represent the real state of things in the United States as a whole. But there has been no reliable contradiction of the facts spoken to by him from his own personal observation. Nor has any reason been assigned for discrediting his description or considering that the area from which his facts were gathered was not representative of the other cities or states. It is stated by Bertrand Russell that as a casual traveller he took some pains to test Judge Lindsey's assertions by questioning young men and that he did not find them inclined to deny his statements of fact. The important place occupied in dramatic literature by sex attraction and love is quite intelligible. But the extraordinary vogue enjoyed by plays depicting sexual anarchy may fairly be taken as some indication not merely of the perversion of public taste, but also of the slackening of the moral fibre in America. The play of Eugene O'Neill called 'A Strange Interlude' which was produced by the Theatre Guild in 1928 not merely passed the scrutiny of the district attorney of New York, but was hailed as the outstanding novelty of the dramatic year and the most interesting and significant contribution made by an American playwright within the memory of living play-goers, and was also awarded the Pulitzer play prize. It is now admitted that the changes which have taken place in America are also noticeable in England, though not perhaps to the same extent. Dean Inge refers to the sympathetic condonation of adultery as a strange phenomenon of modern times in England. The enormous increase in the number of divorces in western countries and especially in America has caused great concern to the religiously minded and the present trend in marriage has been aptly described by a bishop as a a 'tide of consecutive polygamy'.[1]

It is necessary to refer to the causes to which this upheaval of morals in Europe and America has been traced by sociologists. The earliest and most important factor in the disruption of the family was the industrial revolution which drew young people away from their homes in the country and obliged them to live in towns or cities, free from the control and supervision of their parents and from the public opinion of the small circle of neighbours to which they would be subject, if they remained in the country. Living away from their homes, young people were released from the burdens and responsibilities which would have fallen upon them as members of a family under the parental roof. They had more leisure and greater opportunities for coming in contact with a larger number of young people of the opposite sex. While their earnings were probably sufficient for their own maintenance, they were inadequate to enable them to maintain a separate house or support a family.

The postponement of marriage till the parties should become economically self-sufficient imposed an excessive strain upon the emotional life of young people and placed them under the dilemma of asceticism or illicit intimacies. Marriage and sexual expression were denied to many people just at the time when the urgency of the biological instinct was strongest. The great increase in the

[1] V. F. Calverton: *The Bankruptcy of Marriage*, p. 75.

numbers of people who remained unmarried either from want of means or from an unwillingness to forego the freedom and pleasures of single life was not favourable to the strict observance of the moral code. Though monogamy is the Christian ideal of marriage, it has never been strictly observed by the male sex in Europe and the infidelity of men to the marriage vow has been viewed with leniency both by the law and by public opinion. It has been observed by some writers that though modern marriage in Europe and America is monogamy in theory, it has in practice been polygamy for the man. The obligation has, however, lain heavily on women and been enforced by public opinion with the same severity as among Hindus. This double standard of sexual morals is condemned by the rigorous moralists as well as the humanitarian men of letters whose sympathies are aroused by the harshness with which society visits the lapses of women, especially when they have been followed by pregnancy.

The emancipation of women, their claim to equality of rights and treatment and their objection to a double standard of morals for the two sexes have also operated in the direction of giving women the same freedom that has been hitherto granted to men. Equality might be promoted either by curtailment of the freedom of men or by enlargement of the freedom of women. The latter alternative has evidently been found to be more practicable than the former. Bertrand Russell is of opinion that "the modern feminists are no longer anxious as the feminists of thirty years ago to curtail the 'vices' of men; they ask rather that what is permitted to men shall be permitted also to them."[1] According to an American writer, the 'sowing of wild oats' is no longer the particular prerogative of the man.[2]

Another direction in which the emancipation of women has influenced their conduct is to stimulate their desire for economic independence and their wish to compete with men in all occupations except those for which they are physically unfit. The desire for a professional career is in many cases inconsistent with the obligations of married life as hitherto understood, more especially when the occupations of the husband and wife might require them to reside in different places. The professional woman is thus disinclined to undertake obligations which might deprive her of her career and interfere with her prospects of economic independence. The new woman considers that she should not be forced to make a choice between the renunciation of her economic independence and the renunciation of all opportunities for the expression of her sex instincts. Further, the domestic burdens of the family which ordinarily fall to the lot of the wife involve an amount of drudgery which the modern woman is unwilling to undertake and which is inconsistent with the pursuit of the recreations, diversions or forms of social service which she has learnt to prize.

[1] *Marriage and Morals*, p. 69.
[2] V. F. Calverton: *The Bankruptcy of Marriage*, p. 94.

The operation of these inducements to avoid marriage is powerfully assisted by the modern discovery of contraceptives which offer to the unmarried woman a ready means of obtaining sex gratification outside marriage and without the risk of parenthood.

Then again the laws relating to divorce either offer too great facilities which are a temptation to frequent dissolution of marriage and a loss of regard for its permanence or are so stringent as to refuse relief where justly needed and deter the modern woman from marriage. Individual development and advancement are becoming the goal of educated women and Prof. Ruth Reed voices the demand of the new women for new family forms which would enable them to achieve motherhood without lifelong association and for love without the definite mode of life and activity demanded by conventional marriage.[1]

Whatever differences of opinion there may be as to the extent to which the new conceptions of sex morality have obtained ascendancy over the new generation and have been exercising a disruptive influence upon the family as an institution, there can be no doubt that the changes which have been set in motion have been sufficiently serious to create a feeling of alarm in the minds of large numbers of thoughtful people among the older generation. Do these changes augur ill or otherwise for the well-being of society? Is it likely that the transformation of moral ideas will

[1] *The Modern Family*, pp. 27, 41, 42.

go on unchecked and end in anarchy and disaster, or is it likely to be arrested? Those who believe in the institutions of marriage and family cannot afford to shut their eyes to the defects which have disclosed themselves in the working of these institutions and which are responsible for not a little maladjustment and avoidable unhappiness and suffering. They are, however, convinced that both these institutions are essential for the welfare of the human race and that stability in the relations between the sexes must be sought by some process of adaptation and re-orientation. It has been suggested by some writers who have studied the new phenomena of sex life in the West and the numerous irregularities and departures from conventional standards that a system of companionate marriage should be recognised which would render the institution less irksome and more flexible. It is too early to pronounce any opinion upon the results of the great experiment which is being tried in Russia in the sphere of family and property. It has been stated by a very competent observer that though Bolshevism does not exact any obligation to marital fidelity and there is no obstacle to the dissolution of marriages either by mutual consent or at the free will and pleasure of either party, promiscuity is now severely reprobated by public opinion in Russia.[1] Proceeding as it does upon the necessity for a complete overthrow of these two institutions, the experiment is not likely to throw any helpful

[1] *See* Maurice Hindus: *The Great Offensive,* Chapter VII, *passim.*

light upon the problem of the preservation of these institutions in a re-vitalised form.

The questions which occur to us in India are whether the changes which have taken place in the moral ideals of the West are also likely to manifest themselves in India, and if so, whether it is possible to avert them. Optimists may suggest that these new ideas of morality are foreign to the spirit of Hinduism and that firmly attached as we are to the sacredness of the institutions of family and marriage, we are not likely to succumb to the influences which have brought about the new morality in the West. But these people are not aware of the previous history of moral ideas in the West and imagine that it is altogether different from that of the East. The ideas which prevailed on the subject of sex relations during the Victorian epoch in England and America were hardly different from those prevalent in India. Though monogamy was the ideal in these two countries, the standards practically enforced were different as between the two sexes. While a large measure of laxity was allowed to the stronger sex, it was enforced against women with the same rigour as it is in India. The extremely prudish notions of decency and propriety which prevailed among women in Victorian England and in America have been described in numerous books on the domestic manners of the last century. The display of her ankles by a woman was regarded as indecent. She was not allowed to go without an escort in public. It is stated by Harriet Martineau that she believed the coronation of Queen Victoria was the only occasion on which a lady could be allowed alone in public without an escort. The author of a book on the domestic manners of the Americans was informed by an American lady that they were not used to picnics and that it was considered very indelicate for ladies and gentlemen to sit down together on the grass. There is a fundamental similarity of human nature whether in the West or in the East, and the main differences now observable in the manners and morals of England and India seem to be largely due to the lag in our economic and educational progress. But we are trying to cover the distance that separates the two civilisations and treading the same path towards economic progress that has been already traversed by the nations of the West. It may even be said that we are in a feverish hurry to catch up Western nations. The pressure of economic conditions compels many young women to seek employment away from their homes and go through the necessary course of education and training. Apart from the necessity of earning a livelihood which does not press on all women alike, their education necessarily enlarges their mental horizon, increases the range of their interests in life and imbues them with new ideals and new ambitions. The political equality of women was achieved in England after a long and arduous struggle. Women in India have obtained it without any fight and without even asking for it. There has been no disposition in India to deny the eligibility of women to sit in the legislatures or local bodies or to enter the public services or to enter any of the professions. In fact, several women have been serving as members of the legislatures or local bodies or as magistrates and given a good account of themselves. Their claims to education have been recognised by their parents and the government and those who are well-to-do are ready and willing to give the benefits of a collegiate education to their daughters. Some advanced persons have gone the length of advocating the co-education of girls during adolescence either from a desire to follow what they consider to be the latest western fashions or from a belief that the best way of rendering youth immune against the attractions and temptations of sex is by the promotion of familiarity during adolescence or from a belief that opportunities for social contact and friendship would enable youth to form a sounder judgment of the characters of persons of the opposite sex. The girl-students in a certain college have also expressed a preference for co-education on the ground that the presence of male students helps to relieve the dullness of college life. It has also been alleged that college girls in a certain part of India appreciate the pleasure of dancing with their male fellow-students. The necessary result of the desire for higher education has been to postpone the age of marriage of women, and several of those who have entered the professions have either decided not to marry or indefinitely put off marriage. Grown-up girls are often sent to distant places away from their homes to complete their education. No restrictions by way of escort are considered to be necessary or practicable and the girls become more and more capable of taking care of themselves without any chaperon. The married women of the new generation among the upper classes have organised clubs for recreation and have formed associations for carrying on various forms of social service, and they take part in public meetings and are prepared to participate in the discussion of political, social, educational or economic questions. They run their own magazines for the advocacy of women's cause and are ready to travel long distances to attend conferences for the discussion of matters of special interest to women. They have been moved by the spirit of patriotism and are ready to face the consequences of political agitation and undergo suffering. The ideals of culture, social service and nationalism which our educated womenfolk place before themselves are in no way different in kind from those which actuate our men or the educated women of the West. The number of women of the educated classes to whom the above description applies is still extremely small compared with the population. But the ripple that has been caused on the surface of the placidly stagnant life of the Indian woman is bound to spread in larger and larger circles and the intellectual ferment caused by the inrush of new ideas is bound to stir their nature to greater depths. The portals of Western literature and science are open to Indian youth and it would be impossible to prevent the penetration of Western ideals of life and conduct. What the result of this impact of Western ideals upon the Hindu mind will be and whether it will react in the same way as the minds of Western youth have reacted or in a different manner it is hard to forecast. That these developments in the ideas and activities of educated young women have enabled them to lead a fuller life of varied interests must be conceded. But is it reasonable to expect that those who may be inclined or obliged to avoid matrimony will all be prepared to submit to starvation of one of the most imperious instincts of human life?

That the consequences of the new ideals regarding the relations between the sexes and the members of the family have been harmful in some respects in the West will probably be the general opinion of Hindu society. Having regard to the new ideas and other factors in our present conditions which are moulding the lives of the younger generation in India, is it possible for us to feel secure that the evils which have arisen in the West will not also arise here? If there is a likelihood of similar changes in our ideals, is it possible to counteract their influence, and if so, by what means? Reactionary conservatives may suggest a reversion to the old policy of denying all education, or at least higher education, to women and keeping them under the subjection of men. But such proposals are preposterous and it would be impossible to deprive women of their votes or their freedom or their right to education. Some may be inclined to think that even though it might not be possible to shut out knowledge of other kinds, this country should follow the reactionary policy of Roman Catholic countries and strictly exclude from this country any knowledge of birth-control. Like other scientific inventions and discoveries the methods of birth-control are capable of being put to bad as well as good uses and it would be absurd to deprive the people of the country of a remedy not merely against the evils of over-population, but also against the evils arising from excessive child-bearing in the shape of injury to the health of mothers and children and want of means for the proper nourishment, rearing and education of children.

India has long suffered from the evils of child-marriage, but it would be equally a mistake to postpone marriage to a late age. It is now perceived in the West that the lengthening of the interval between the time when biological instincts make themselves vigorously felt and the age when a person is economically in a position to set up a house for himself and bring up a family has been productive of great unhappiness and grave injury to morals. In cases where the financial resources of the husband and the wife would not enable them to support the additional burden of children and render them disinclined to marry, it would be legitimate to use contraceptives for the purpose of avoiding any additions to the family. Even a religious moralist must concede that the postponement of procreation under such circumstances is a smaller evil than nominal celibacy and sexual immorality. I should be disposed to regard the postponement of marriage beyond 25 for men and 21 for women as very undesirable. It is far from my intention to dogmatise upon this subject, but I may add that my view is supported by what I have heard from medical men that the optimum age for the first child-birth for Indian women is between 18 and 25.

While the economic independence of women is desirable on many grounds, it seems very unwise to encourage the ambition for a professional career in women, except perhaps in those who may be specially gifted for particular callings. The old Hindu ideal of the woman as the maker of the home which considers the position of the wife and mother the most sacred and honourable in society is one which we cannot afford to abandon. It must be the ideal of female education in India to impress upon the minds of girls the exalted Hindu ideal of woman as wife and mother. The reaction of Hindu women to the influences of the new age can be largely determined by the moral education given to them during the most plastic period of their life, by the notions, impulses and inhibitions implanted in their minds during this period. There is no need to fear that the highest ideals of womanhood pictured to us in Hinduism will be found inadequate to the requirements of a rational, wholesome and happy life even under modern conditions. The Hindu conception of marriage may appear somewhat prosaic and unsentimental to those whose minds have been fed upon the romantic notions of love which figure so largely in modern English fiction. Romances are unfortunately built upon illusions and do not last in this world of work, stress and realities. But the assumptions upon which the institution of marriage is based are psychologically well founded and hold good in the West and in the East. As pointed out by Walter Lippmann in his *Preface to Morals,* "given an initial attraction, a common social background, common responsibilities and the conviction that the relationship is permanent, compatibility in marriage can normally be achieved. It is precisely this that the prevailing sentimentality about love denies. It assumes that marriages are made in heaven, that compatibility is instinctive, a mere coincidence, that happy unions are, in the last analysis, lucky accidents in which two people who happen to suit each other happen to have met. The convention of marriage rests on an interpretation of human nature which does not confuse the subjective feeling of the lovers that their passion is unique, with the brutal but objective fact that, had they never met, each of them would in all probability have found a lover who was just as unique. 'Love' says Mr. Santayana, 'is indeed much less exacting than it thinks itself. Nine-tenths of its cause are in the lover for one-tenth that may be in the object. Were the latter not accidentally at hand, an almost identical passion would probably have been felt for someone else; for, although with acquaintance the quality of an attachment naturally adapts itself to the person loved, and makes that person its standard and ideal, the first assault and mysterious glow of the passion is much the same for every object.' . . The fallacy of the popular conception of romantic love is in the failure to realise that compatibility is a process and not an accident and that it depends upon the maturing of instinctive desire by adaptation to the whole nature of the other person and to the common concerns of the pair of lovers."[1] How much can be accomplished by a scientifically devised system of education and how it is possible to give a strong bias in any desired direction can be seen from the success of the efforts of the Bolsheviks in Russia in completely uprooting all the old ideals and replacing them by new ideals, new ambitions and new enthusiasms. The fashionable ideal of self-expression and self-development will have to be replaced by the ideal of self-control and the ordered and harmonious development of our faculties and impulses.

In emphasising the necessity of preserving the institution of marriage I have not overlooked the fact that the marriage laws of the Hindus are, like other systems of law made by the male sex, more liberal to men than to women. In the chapter on marriage I have pointed out how while the older Hindu law allowed a dissolution of marriage in certain cases, the later law-givers have generally denied the right to women and allowed

[1] P. 309 ff.

the husband to supersede the wife on various grounds. If the principle of equality between the sexes is to be carried out in the personal law, it is necessary to provide the remedy of a dissolution to women as well as men in cases where the maintenance of the legal bond is productive of grave hardship. Here we approach a subject of great difficulty and extreme complexity which has a bearing not merely on the happiness of individuals, but upon the well-being of society. While it is necessary to avoid undue facilities for dissolution of the tie, it is equally necessary to avoid too great stringency and obviate hardship. That some measure of relaxation in the existing law is necessary will be conceded by all reasonable people. It is not possible for me here to discuss the grounds on which relief should be awarded. I will only advert to the fact that the progressive state of Baroda has realised the necessity for legislation and has passed a law for the dissolution of Hindu marriages on certain grounds.

So long as private property is recognised by the law and the love of children continues to be one of the deep-seated instincts of humanity, it is reasonably certain that the family will continue to survive as an institution, notwithstanding the efforts of the modern state under socialistic influence to undertake several of the social services performed by the family, such as the nursing of the children, the education of the young and the support of the aged, infirm, disabled or unemployed members of the family.

The idea of private property is closely bound up with the institution of family. The attacks indirectly made upon private property by the action of the state under the influence of socialistic ideas have not yet gone the length of advocating its abolition except in the case of land. Various proposals have been made for nationalising many industrial undertakings. But except in Russia and by the communists, war has not been made upon the conception of private property. The Russian revolution has deliberately and systematically aimed at the extirpation of the idea of private property and it seems to have almost succeeded in tearing up the institution by its roots and in bringing up a new generation which seems to regard private property as a sin and a crime. Liberty and equality were two of the watchwords of the French Revolution. Since the abolition of the monarchical form of government in many of the countries of Europe, the love of political liberty has receded into the background and the passion for equality appears to be the dominant impulse of humanity at the present time. An equality of privation is a more attractive ideal than wealth with inequality of distribution. Whether the price exacted by the Russian revolution for the achievement of the ideal of equality is not too great and whether the Bolshevik experiment is likely to be conducive to human liberty and happiness, it is yet too early to prophesy.

It is sometimes said that Bolshevism can never take root in India with its multitude of small agricultural holdings and poor peasants. But those who imagine that this country is proof against the danger of an economic revolution are apt to overlook two circumstances which have played an important part in history. The great mass of poverty and unemployment offer a favourable soil for the seeds of revolution. While those who are in possession of property are generally disunited, inert and wanting in energy and enthusiasm, the have-nots and revolutionaries are far more capable of combination and sustained effort and vigorous offensive. The history of the Russian revolution teaches the lesson that a compact and well-organised minority inspired by zeal can overcome the opposition of an unorganised majority however vast, and succeed in establishing itself in power. This is not the time or place to enter into any discussion of the possibilities of an economic revolution in this country. But I have referred to it merely for the purpose of hinting how enormous changes in our moral conceptions are sure to be brought about by changes in the social or economic order. Virtues may lose their importance or cease to be virtues and new ideals of conduct may take the place of old. There is reason to fear that the beautiful ideals of filial love and affection, of affection between brothers, of respect for elders and especially those of the family, of conjugal constancy and of the support of aged parents are losing their influence upon the conduct of persons. The time perhaps is not far off (and I should indeed deplore the day) when the new generation may become incapable even of appreciating the beauty of the ideals depicted in our national epics.

This train of reflection is apt to produce a sense of despondency and a feeling that there is nothing to be done except to fold our hands and allow ourselves to drift at the mercy of the winds and waves. But I feel that we should look for guidance in the true spirit of the Hindu religion and philosophy. I may end with a quotation from Washburn Hopkins's *Ethics of India*: "What India needs is to realise itself, to broaden out her spiritual heritage until it meets the further requirements of this later age, not to rest upon the foundation already nobly erected by her own saints and scholars, but to continue to build along the same inspiring lines. The Hindu epic says 'every man is king in his own house' (*sarvas sve sve gṛhe rājā*) and every one likes to feel that one is living in a spiritual house of one's own, of which one is hereditary lord. It is well for the Hindu to be able to think: This is our spiritual and ethical heritage; here is the word of our own saint, who says, 'bless them that curse you'; of our own sage, who declares that 'the Vedas do not purify an immoral man'; here is the injunction, taught us long ago, to define a nobleman as one who is noble of soul; here is the statement that God is a spirit devoid of all evil and that righteousness is divine; here is the commandment to pity the unfortunate and to seek, not condescendingly but sympathetically, to do good to all."[1]

[1] P. 258.

INDEX.

A

B

D

E

F

G

H

S

Y

PRINTED AT THE MADRAS LAW JOURNAL PRESS, MYLAPORE, MADRAS.